PRAISE FOR *MURDE...*
MOONSHINE, AND...

"Harrington's book is priceless—I read it in one sitting and laughed till I cried. The humor is cutting and relevant in a way that often is missing from Christian writing. I appreciate that he doesn't shy away from complicated relationships and questionable decisions in the stories found in the Scriptures. Five stars!"

— **Amanda Martinez Beck**, author of *Lovely: How I Learned to Embrace the Body God Gave Me*

"What *Murder-Bears* gets right is that the best way to take the Bible seriously is not to take it so seriously. While its purpose may be divine, the Bible is a deeply human book, full of deeply human things. Human things like farts and over-the-top murders and butts and ding-dongs."

— **Benito Cereno**, cohost of *Apocrypals,* writer for *Tales from the Bully Pulpit* and *The Tick: New Series*

"We've grown bored of the socially acceptable version of the Bible. That's why we need someone like Luke Harrington who is somehow able to see the Bible for what it is: a book full of gross, disgusting, scandalous incidents. By forcing us to reckon with the more unbecoming details that get left out of our children's story Bibles, Luke reclaims the Bible for adults and teenage boys everywhere."

— **Richard Clark**, former editor for *Christianity Today*, former editor-in-chief of *Christ and Pop Culture*

"The Bible is many wonderful things, including *weird*. We need more weird writers writing about it. And I say that as the highest compliment because Luke writes with verve and fun and style, and there aren't many who can do that. He makes us see weirdness in a fresh way, which, as it turns out, is a beautiful way."

— **Brant Hansen**, radio host and author of *The Truth About Us, Unoffendable,* and *Blessed Are the Misfits*

"Finally someone has written the definitive work about homicidal animals, divine poop, and foreskins. But not only that, Luke Harrington has also redeemed these disparate ideas by explaining and celebrating their correlation to the Holy Scripture. I wish all books about the Bible were this much fun."

— **Knox McCoy**, author of *The Wondering Years* and *All Things Reconsidered*

"As I was reading this book, my eight-year-old wandered into my office and started reading over my shoulder. 'He's very connected to poop,' he commented. It was an accurate observation. But there was more than just poop. Or butts. Or man-eating bears. Or circumcision jokes. Beneath the edgy hilarity I saw a real affection for the Good Book and the God who inspired it. Harrington just better hope that God has a sense of humor—or those bears might be coming for him."

— **Drew Dyck**, author of *Your Future Self Will Thank You: Secrets to Self-Control from the Bible and Brain Science* and *Yawning at Tigers: You Can't Tame God, so Stop Trying*

"A good book, from what I am told. Of course I haven't read it—I am too busy being an Evangelical Thought Leader and engaging the culture with hot takes—but Luke has assured me that if you read it, there is a 63 percent chance you will get holier, 50 percent of the time."

— **Matthew Pierce**, cohost of *Fun Sexy Bible Time*, author of *Homeschool Sex Machine: Babes, Bible Quiz, and the Clinton Years*

"*Murder-Bears, Moonshine, and Mayhem* is like a comedy act and a seminary course rolled into one. I don't think I've ever read a book that had me laughing out loud and looking at the footnotes as many times as this one. Luke Harrington gives the grit and gore of the Bible its due—and masterfully shows how even these point us to grace and to the gospel."

— **Karen Swallow Prior**, author of *On Reading Well: Finding the Good Life through Great Books* and *Fierce Convictions: The Extraordinary Life of Hannah More—Poet, Reformer, Abolitionist*

"The beloved scriptures we call the Bible contain powerful truths that have changed hearts and minds for centuries. But this book also contains all manner of provocative, disturbing, unusual, and hilarious accounts of living life on earth as a human. In *Murder-Bears, Moonshine, and Mayhem*, Luke T. Harrington dissects some of the strangest and most confusing biblical narratives with his signature wit. Harrington masterfully weaves together sharp theological insights with comedic commentary. (Don't skip the footnotes.) In acknowledging and sharing a laugh over the Bible's quirks, readers will be awed anew at God's love and long-suffering for humanity and discover the humor laced throughout the human project."

— **Erin M. Straza**, author of *Comfort Detox: Finding
Freedom from Habits That Bind You*

MURDER-BEARS, MOONSHINE, AND MAYHEM.

STRANGE STORIES FROM THE BIBLE TO LEAVE YOU AMUSED, BEMUSED, AND (HOPEFULLY) INFORMED

LUKE T. HARRINGTON

W PUBLISHING GROUP

AN IMPRINT OF THOMAS NELSON

Published in Nashville, Tennessee, by W Publishing, an imprint of Thomas Nelson.

Thomas Nelson titles may be purchased in bulk for educational, business, fundraising, or sales promotional use. For information, please e-mail SpecialMarkets@ ThomasNelson.com.

Unless otherwise noted, Scripture quotations are taken from the ESV® Bible (The Holy Bible, English Standard Version®). Copyright © 2001 by Crossway, a publishing ministry of Good News Publishers. Used by permission. All rights reserved.

Scripture quotations marked GNT are from the Good News Translation in Today's English Version—Second Edition. Copyright 1992 by American Bible Society. Used by permission.

Scripture quotations marked GW are from *God's Word*®. Copyright © 1995 God's Word to the Nations. Used by permission of Baker Publishing Group. All rights reserved.

Scripture quotations marked KJV are from the King James Version. Public domain.

Scripture quotations marked NASB are from New American Standard Bible®. Copyright © 1960, 1962, 1963, 1968, 1971, 1972, 1973, 1975, 1977, 1995 by The Lockman Foundation. Used by permission. (www.Lockman.org)

Scripture quotations marked NIV are from the Holy Bible, New International Version®, NIV®. Copyright © 1973, 1978, 1984, 2011 by Biblica, Inc.® Used by permission of Zondervan. All rights reserved worldwide. www.Zondervan.com. The "NIV" and "New International Version" are trademarks registered in the United States Patent and Trademark Office by Biblica, Inc.®

Scripture quotations marked NLT are from the Holy Bible, New Living Translation. © 1996, 2004, 2007, 2013, 2015 by Tyndale House Foundation. Used by permission of Tyndale House Publishers, Inc., Carol Stream, Illinois 60188. All rights reserved.

Scripture quotations marked ISV are from the Holy Bible: International Standard Version® Release 2.0. Copyright © 1996–2013 by the ISV Foundation. Used by permission of Davidson Press, LLC. All rights reserved internationally.

Any Internet addresses, phone numbers, or company or product information printed in this book are offered as a resource and are not intended in any way to be or to imply an endorsement by Thomas Nelson, nor does Thomas Nelson vouch for the existence, content, or services of these sites, phone numbers, companies, or products beyond the life of this book.

ISBN 978-0-7852-3444-9 (TP)
ISBN 978-0-7852-3445-6 (eBook)

Library of Congress Cataloging-in-Publication Data

Library of Congress Control Number: 2020006593

Printed in the United States of America

20 21 22 23 24   LSC   10 9 8 7 6 5 4 3 2 1

For my dad,
who taught me to love terrible jokes.
And also the Bible, I guess.

Of making many books there is no end, and much study is a weariness of the flesh.

—ECCLESIASTES 12:12B

Buy my book! Buy my book!

—JAY SHERMAN, *THE CRITIC*

CONTENTS

INTRODUCTION

I Was a Teenage PK

I'm going to open this book with a memory.

I'm probably about ten years old, sitting on my father's lap in the glow of a small, yellowing floor lamp that fights hard against the setting sun. He smells like coffee and his voice is warm gravel. He's reading to me:

> He went up from there to Bethel, and while he was going up on the way, some small boys came out of the city and jeered at him, saying, "Go up, you baldhead! Go up, you baldhead!" And he turned around, and when he saw them, he cursed them in the name of the LORD. **And two she-bears came out of the woods and tore forty-two of the boys.** (2 Kings 2:23–24)

And I'm thinking, "I just found my life verse."[1]

/ / /

---

1. If you don't know what a life verse is, ask an evangelical friend to explain it to you.

This book is something of a story, and that story begins with my father. My father is a pastor—actually, it would be more accurate to say that he's a *minister*. He's ordained for ministry in a tiny Presbyterian denomination, but, except for a handful of years when I was a kid, he's never actually pastored a church. It's possible that a pulpit gig would come with a bit more prestige, but my dad's never really been interested in prestige;[2] instead, he's devoted his life to student ministry, spending his days drinking coffee and chatting about Christianity with international students at my own alma mater, the University of Nebraska–Lincoln. He's also, as you might imagine a minister to be, fairly passionate about the Bible.

I'm not sure if it was he or my mother who instituted nightly Bible stories when I was a kid, but I *do* remember that he had a unique way of defending them when we began to complain—as we inevitably did. "Uuuuuuuuuugggggghhhh, Daaaaaaaaaaaaaaaaaddddd," we'd say (because it was the totally radical '90s and all the cool kids talked like this), "the Bible is soooooooooooo booooooooorrrrinnngggg."

Given how saccharine the average children's Bible storybook is, we weren't exactly *wrong* to feel this way. In the face of such whining, a lesser parent would have given up, or announced, "Too bad, we're doing this anyway," or thundered, "HOW DARE YOU SAY THAT ABOUT THE WORD OF THE LORD!" and then chained us to our beds like a Stephen King villain. My dad, however, took our complaints as a challenge.

"The Bible is boring, eh?" he'd say. "Is *this* boring?" And he would crack open the Bible to a story about kids getting mauled

---

2. Nor have I, which is why I'm sitting here writing a book on the butt jokes in the Bible.

by bears, or a concubine getting diced up, or a prophet baking poop bread. Then, having been thoroughly traumatized, we would all be forced to admit that the Bible is many things, but it is *not* boring.

/ / /

As it turns out, there's a *lot* of weird stuff in the Bible. Grisly violence, depraved sex acts, poop jokes (*so many poop jokes*)—even a handful of verses that Calvinists like. If we're being honest with ourselves, though, is it *that* surprising to see weird stuff in the Bible? After all, *everything* is weird to *someone, somewhere*. What people consider weird is almost entirely determined by their culture, and—brace yourself—it turns out the Bible comes from a culture different from our own.[3] To the sufficiently narrow-minded, *everything* is weird. And hey, good for them, because they get to giggle a lot.

This book is for those people—the ones who never get tired of giggling about poop, especially when it's mentioned in the Bible. I wrote it because I like the Bible, and because I like giggling about poop. I want to be clear, though, that I did *not* write it for either of the following reasons:

1. **To ridicule the Bible.** After all, ridiculing things is easy. You take something out of context or paraphrase it badly, and then you wiggle your eyebrows at the peanut gallery. It can be fun, but it's also lazy and it's ultimately pointless—after all, even if you hate the Bible, it's not

---

3. Actually, multiple cultures, over thousands of years. Contrary to common belief, the world was not a stodgy monolith prior to 1960.

going anywhere. So, if you're looking for mockery, go look somewhere else.[4]

2. **To defend or apologize for the Bible.** I think we've probably all met the pew-fillers who will frown on going to an R-rated film but will insist it's *totally different* when the Bible contains explicit material. ("You're taking that out of context!" they'll say, oblivious to the fact that films also have contexts.) I have no desire to be one of those people either—they're often just as obnoxious as the "ridicule the Bible" set.

In short, I think the material here is capable of speaking for itself.[5] There's an old quote from nineteenth-century preacher Charles Spurgeon about how defending Scripture is like defending a lion: You don't have to. You let it out of its cage, and it defends itself.[6] I think he was probably right; despite the best efforts of many over the centuries to soften, censor, or ridicule the Bible, it remains a book that billions have read and found profound meaning in. In other words, it's not a book that everyone likes, but it's clearly doing *something* right. I really don't have an agenda with this book other than to encourage you to consider what that "something" might be.

And yes, part of that "something" is probably poop jokes.

I'm mostly serious about this. If you believe, as I do, that the Bible is God's message for all of humanity, then it makes sense

---

4. I recommend *The Skeptic's Annotated Bible*, which is basically what you'd get if you gave a Bible and a Sharpie to Beavis and Butt-Head.

5. "So why'd you write a book, then, Luke?" "Because this way I get paid."

6. C. H. Spurgeon, "The Lover of God's Law Filled with Peace," in *The Metropolitan Tabernacle Pulpit Sermons*, vol. 34 (London: Passmore & Alabaster, 1888), 42.

that it would have something in it for *everyone*—not just the over-educated theologians, or the prudish old ladies, or the creepy homeschool kids working the Chick-fil-A counter. It's also for the lowbrow types. The poor. The oppressed. The broken. If you believe the stuff that Jesus and the prophets said, it's actually *mostly* for that crowd.

So, yeah, it will have poop jokes.

The *best* poop jokes.

Divine poop jokes.

/ / /

It's been my experience that nearly everyone has a *very* strong opinion about the Bible—what it is, what it means, what we should all think of it—but polls show that something in the neighborhood of 80 percent of people will admit to never having read the whole thing.[7] What if we all stopped forming opinions about the Bible for a second and . . . just read it?

So—let's read it. Starting with the poop jokes.[8]

I hope you enjoy this book. I hope it makes you laugh, and I hope you learn something, and I hope it inspires you to pick up a Bible. But most of all, I hope you'll join me in that chair in my bedroom on my father's lap (but not in a weird way), mouth agape at the secret, strange riches the ancient Scriptures have to offer.

---

7. See, for example, this poll conducted by LifeWay Research in 2016: https://lifewayresearch.com/2017/04/25/lifeway-research-americans-are-fond-of-the-bible-dont-actually-read-it/.

8. I mean, obviously.

I LIKE BIBLICAL BUTTS
AND I CANNOT LIE

Butts, Poop, and More!

Whenever the existence of God[1] is debated, there's an old argument that keeps coming up on the "pro" side called the "teleological argument." Proposed and developed by such great minds as Socrates, St. Thomas Aquinas, and Kirk Cameron (two out of three ain't bad), the argument, at its core, is this:

> Everything in nature appears to serve a clear purpose;
> therefore, it must be designed for that purpose;
> therefore, there must be a *designer*.[2]

---

1. John Duns Scotus, Thomas Aquinas, and others have actually argued that it's a category error to say that God "exists," since God transcends existence and all existence flows from God. But you know what I mean.
2. See Xenophon, *Memorabilia* 1.4; Thomas Aquinas, *Summa Theologica* 1.2.3; and then google "Kirk Cameron banana argument."

Boom. God exists.

An open-and-shut case, right? Haha, no, of course not, because the teleological argument, for all its insight, overlooks a rather obvious question: *Does* everything in nature serve a clear purpose? Not only is nature *itself* evidently purposeless, but it has all sorts of features that seem to serve no purpose at all, like the human appendix, male nipples, and lite jazz music. All too often, the believer will think he has his skeptical opponent on the ropes only for said skeptic to bust out an anatomy textbook or flip the radio over to Smooth Sounds 103, thus rendering the believer defenseless.

It occurs to me, though, that there's a fairly obvious response to this challenge that goes woefully underused: maybe God just has a sense of humor. There's no reason we have to imagine God as an obsessive engineer, fine-tuning the universe into some sort of hyperefficient machine (designed to do . . . what, exactly?). Maybe the Big Guy is also part comedian, filling the earth and the cosmos with things that serve no purpose at all other than to be *hilarious*. Would *you* want to live in a world where something as entertaining as a lite jazz saxophonist with saggy man-nipples and an exploding appendix couldn't exist? I know *I* wouldn't.

Which brings me to butts. After all, what purpose does the human butt serve, aside from being hilarious and helping us look sporty in G-strings? *Yes*, Neil deGrasse Tyson, we're aware that defecation rids the body of toxins and the gluteal muscles are necessary for locomotion, but doesn't it say *something* that our bodies accomplish those things with a device as hilarious as a butt? That we all walk around with a little perpetual comedy machine attached to our bodies, just waiting to inject some hilarity into life with a well-timed fart or an accidental mooning?

I already know what you're going to say: "Obviously, any

reasonable person would find a butt hilarious, but how can we possibly know *God* does? Your addition to the teleological argument is absurd, and you'll die sad and alone!"

Well, first off, that was hurtful. And second, if you doubt that God finds butts funny, all you have to do is *read his book.* What's funny is, of course, always in the eye of the beholder, but you don't have to look far in the Bible before you come across an arguably hilarious instance of a butt, or some poop, or a butt making poop.

For instance:

David to Saul: "I Saw Your Butt (Making Poop)"

Everyone knows the story of David and Goliath, but if you've spent much time reading the Bible, you also know David is one of the Old Testament's A-listers, with countless adventures that sprawl across multiple books. Unlike the Goliath narrative, though, many of these stories are less than Sunday school ready. And yes, many of them involve poop.

There's a rivalry in 1 Samuel between David and King Saul, but it's only a rivalry in the sense that the Lakers and the Clippers have a rivalry. That is to say, only one of them knows about it. Saul is Israel's king, and David is the God-and-country Boy Scout type who just wants to do whatever he can to support his monarch and his motherland. Unfortunately for David, Saul is a relentlessly paranoid politician who's convinced everyone else in the room is out to usurp his throne. This is particularly bad news for David, who as Saul's court musician not only frequently finds himself in the same room as Saul but has *also been prophesied to usurp Saul's throne.*

This all leads Saul to fly into a murderous rage and start chasing David through the countryside. (Actually, that happens multiple times. It's a thing.) At one point, David and his men get tired of all this running-for-their-lives stuff and decide to hide in a cave for a while. Unfortunately, Saul has the same idea. Well, sort of:

> And he came to the sheepcotes by the way, where was a cave; and Saul went in to **cover his feet**: and David and his men remained in the sides of the cave. (1 Samuel 24:3 KJV)

I'm going to be using the English Standard Version of the Bible for most of this book, but here I went with the King James because it uses a more literal translation of the original Hebrew, which (as is frequently the case) is charmingly euphemistic. For the moment, ignore the part about sheepcotes, which I believe are stylish jackets for the discerning ovine gentleman. What I want to talk about is the phrase **"cover his feet."** To **"cover your feet"** means exactly what it says: it means you're covering your feet.

With your pants.

Because you're pooping.

So David and his men are hiding in the back of the cave, Saul comes in and fails to notice them, and then David and friends are trapped in the shadows, watching Saul take a dump. It's an image that's difficult to get out of your mind, no matter how much bleach you pour into your eyes.[3] But the upside for David is that he's literally caught his mortal enemy with his pants down, as his men helpfully point out:

---

3. Insert obligatory legal disclaimer here.

And the men of David said to him, "Here is the day of which the LORD said to you, 'Behold, I will give your enemy into your hand, and you shall do to him as it shall seem good to you.'" (verse 4a)

It's a little hard to think of something more embarrassing than being killed by the guy you were trying to kill, while you were in the middle of pooping, but fortunately for Saul, David remains ever the Boy Scout:

Then David arose and stealthily cut off a corner of Saul's robe. (verse 4b)

So despite his phenomenal good luck, David can't bring himself to do anything beyond a bit of casual property destruction.[4] (I have no idea how close to Poop Ground Zero he has to get to accomplish this, but let's assume it was very close, because that's funnier.) Conscientious as he is, though, he soon starts to feel guilty for doing even *that* much:

And afterward **David's heart struck him**, because he had cut off a corner of Saul's robe. He said to his men, "The LORD forbid that I should do this thing to my lord, the LORD's anointed, to put out my hand against him, seeing he is the LORD's anointed." (verses 5–6)

I mean, calm down, kid. There's such a thing as being too squeaky clean.

---

4. Actually, there's the possibility that this was a bit more than that—it may have symbolically been an attack on Saul's authority. The corners of garments had special significance (Numbers 15:38–39).

Anyway, David tracks Saul down and shows him the robe swatch to prove that (1) he could have killed him if he'd wanted to, and (2) he saw him poop. Saul is so profoundly embarrassed by the whole thing that he promises never to try murdering David again.

Then he tries to murder him again, like, two chapters later. Because that's how Saul rolls.

THAT'S ONE WAY TO DEAL WITH CRAPPY PEOPLE

In the prophecy of Malachi, God rebukes some corrupt priests in an, um, colorful way:

> "Behold, I will rebuke your offspring, and **spread dung on your faces**, the dung of your offerings, and you shall be taken away with it." (Malachi 2:3)

This *kind of* makes sense when you consider that Israel's priests were in charge of sacrificing animals, and animal intestines tend to be full of crap. (Actually, the law of Moses is *full* of very specific instructions about what they can/should do with said crap.) Apparently, these priests were *also* full of crap, and God wanted to let them know this as forcefully as possible.

Ezekiel Bakes Some Poop Bread

In the fourth chapter of Ezekiel, God asks the title character, who's something of a full-time prophet and part-time prop comic, to show the people of Jerusalem just how serious he is about destroying their city (*so* serious, you guys). Step one is apparently to play with blocks. As God puts it:

"And you, son of man, **take a brick** and lay it before you, and engrave on it a city, even Jerusalem. And **put siegeworks against it**, and build a siege wall against it, and cast up a mound against it. Set camps also against it, and plant battering rams against it all around." (Ezekiel 4:1–2)

I'm not 100 percent sure how to lay siege to a brick, but I'm fairly certain ten-year-old me would have loved it. In any case, it fails to get the point across, because a couple of verses later God is telling Ezekiel to try something else:

"Then **lie on your left side**, and place the punishment of the house of Israel upon it . . . **390 days**, equal to the number of the years of their punishment. **So long shall you bear the punishment** of the house of Israel." (verses 4–5)

Naturally, Ezekiel wonders what he's supposed to eat while he's spending more than an entire year acquiring bedsores, but God's got that part covered as well:

"And you, take wheat and barley, beans and lentils, millet and emmer, and put them into a single vessel and make your bread from them. . . . And you shall eat it as a barley cake, **baking it in their sight on human dung**." (verses 9a, 12)

In other words, take the trash grains nobody wants to eat, bake them over your own flaming crap (or . . . *somebody's* flaming crap), and then eat the whole greasy, *E. coli*–soaked mess. And while "lying around and eating literal garbage" is what we call "the weekend" in America, at the time it was quite an insult. Ezekiel isn't about to take it lying down:

> Then I said, "Ah, Lord GOD! Behold, **I have never defiled myself**. From my youth up till now I have never eaten what died of itself or was torn by beasts, nor has tainted meat come into my mouth." (verse 14)

I have to tip my hat to Ezekiel here. It's (apparently) not eating crap-baked garbage per se that bothers him; it's just that it's not kosher under the Mosaic dietary laws. God rolls his eyes, mutters "Geez, why do I get stuck with all the pious yahoos?"[5] and then gives Ezekiel the concession he's (apparently) looking for:

> Then he said to me, "See, **I assign to you cow's dung instead of human dung**, on which you may prepare your bread." (verse 15)

The compromise is to still eat the same bread, and still bake it over poop, but just use cow poop instead—a compromise that Ezekiel seems fine with. If I were Ezekiel, I would have pointed out that this compromise was *literally bull crap*, but I guess that's why Ezekiel got to be a prophet and I didn't.

Let me be clear, though: this whole demonstration isn't just

---

5. I mean, I assume.

a weird excuse for kosher coprophagia.[6] If you're confused about the point God is trying to make, you can read the next verse:

> Moreover, he said to me, "Son of man, behold, **I will break the supply of bread in Jerusalem**. They shall eat bread by weight and with anxiety, and they shall drink water by measure and in dismay." (verse 16)

In other words, the subtext here is "Hey, look at the trash bread you'll be eating while your city is under siege." If you don't know what a siege is, and you're too lazy to pick up a dictionary, it's when an attacking army blocks access to a city so that food and other resources (like firewood) can't get in. It's excruciating for the city dwellers, it's mind-numbingly boring for the invaders, and it very rarely involves Steven Seagal dramatically tying back his ponytail. If you're trapped in the city, it usually means starving until you become desperate enough to throw whatever scraps of food you can find into a pot and cook it however you can, as Ezekiel does.

That would apparently be news, though, to anyone at the modern-day Food for Life Baking Co., who will cheerfully sell you a popular product they call "Ezekiel 4:9 Bread." It's made with all six ingredients listed in the passage and possibly baked over human feces. (I mean, the promotional materials never say it *isn't*.)[7] It's almost like they just decided to open the Bible to a random verse and then base a product on it, which will

---

6. Who needs an excuse, right?
7. For more information on Ezekiel 4:9 bread, visit the Food for Life website: https://www.foodforlife.com/about_us/ezekiel-49.

sound entirely plausible to anyone familiar with the evangelical-industrial marketing complex.

It's kind of too bad they didn't open their Bibles to a different passage about siege food, though, or else we could head over to Whole Foods right now and pick up some donkey-head-and-dove-poop meatloaf:

> And there was a great famine in Samaria, as they besieged it, until **a donkey's head** was sold for eighty shekels of silver, and **the fourth part of a kab of dove's dung** for five shekels of silver. (2 Kings 6:25)

Or some boiled toddlers:

> And the king asked her, "What is your trouble?" She answered, "This woman said to me, 'Give your son, that we may eat him today, and we will eat my son tomorrow.' **So we boiled my son and ate him.** And on the next day I said to her, 'Give your son, that we may eat him.' But she has hidden her son." (verses 28–29)

Or just . . . this:

> But Rabshakeh said, Hath my master sent me to thy master and to thee to speak these words? hath he not sent me to the men that sit upon the wall, that they may **eat their own dung, and drink their own piss** with you? (Isaiah 36:12 KJV)

And yes, I deliberately used the King James again there so I could sneak the word "piss" into a Christian book. You're welcome.

REAR WINDOW, STARRING CHARLTON HESTON

In Exodus chapter 33, Moses asks God to show him his full glory. God says, "Um, you'll die if I do that, but . . ."

> And the LORD said, "Behold, there is a place by me where you shall stand on the rock, and while my glory passes by I will put you in a cleft of the rock, and **I will cover you with my hand** until I have passed by. Then I will take away my hand, and **you shall see my back,** but my face shall not be seen." (Exodus 33:21–23)

And honestly, this raises far more questions than it answers. How big are God's hands? How much less impressive is his back than his front? Is God the anti-Kardashian?

Steal the Ark, Get Hemorrhoids

And speaking of war having weird consequences for people's butts, let's talk about the time the Philistines stole the ark of the covenant. You remember the ark of the covenant, right? From *Raiders of the Lost Ark*? In 1 Samuel, the Philistines steal it from the Israelites, and it doesn't work out super well for them. Specifically, for their butts.

It starts when Israel decides to bring the ark into battle:

And when the people came to the camp, the elders of Israel said, "Why has the LORD defeated us today before the

Philistines? **Let us bring the ark of the covenant** of the Lord
here from Shiloh, **that it may come among us and save us**
from the power of our enemies." (1 Samuel 4:3)

You'll recall from that Indiana Jones movie that the Nazis think
the ark is some sort of superweapon that will make their armies
unstoppable, but in the end it just melts said Nazis' faces off.
Israel is making the same basic mistake here, trying to use it as
a magic enemy-defeating machine. The ark, though, is a symbol
of God's presence, not a guarantee of his favor—and it proves
worse than useless to Israel. The Philistines not only defeat them
soundly but also carry the ark away as booty.[8]

They take it back to the city of Ashdod and place it in their
temple next to their own god, Dagon, because gods are collectible, right? As it turns out, though, God isn't huge into being
treated like a Beanie Baby:[9]

And when the people of Ashdod rose early the next day,
behold, **Dagon had fallen face downward** on the ground
before the ark of the Lord. (5:3a)

They wake up and see their god literally bowing down to the ark
they just brought home as a trophy. There's a clear message being
sent here that the God of Israel is not one to be trifled with. The only
real option is to pack up the ark and take it back to Israel, which—

So they took Dagon and **put him back in his place.** (verse 3b)

---

8. Heh.
9. Note to my editor: Beanie Baby jokes are still funny, right? Have someone
   look into that.

Or just shrug and act like nothing happened. That works too.

> But when they rose early on the next morning, behold, Dagon had fallen face downward on the ground before the ark of the LORD, and **the head of Dagon and both his hands were lying cut off** on the threshold. Only the trunk of Dagon was left to him. (verse 4)

At this point God isn't likely to win any awards for subtlety, but the Philistines still aren't getting the message, so he ups the ante and lets loose a plague. Specifically, a plague on their butts:

> And it was so, that, after they had carried [the ark] about, the hand of the LORD was against the city with a very great destruction: and he smote the men of the city, both small and great, and they had **emerods in their secret parts**. (verse 9 KJV)

I'm quoting again from the King James here because it uses a word you don't see in any other Bible translation, or, for that matter, almost anywhere in the English language: **emerods**. Most modern translations just say "boils" or "tumors" in this verse, and in fact the Hebrew word is *ophalim*, which is probably best rendered "swellings."[10] The (apparent) frat boys behind the KJV, however, decided to get creative and use an old-timey word for hemorrhoids. There's a whole, big, boring etymological explanation

---

10. Samuel Kottek, "Medicine in Ancient Hebrew and Jewish Cultures," in *Medicine Across Cultures*, ed. Helaine Selin (Berlin: Springer Science & Business Media, 2003), 305–24.

for why it's spelled **"emerods"** here,[11] but if you squint and say **"emerod"** in a funny voice, you'll see it's basically the same word.

In truth, the original Hebrew word is so vague that there's no way to know the true nature of the plague inflicted on the Philistines (though it was probably still preferable to having their faces melted off, so there's that). Modern scholars have suggested that *ophalim* could refer to anything from tumors[12] to the bubonic plague[13] to the bites of camel spiders.[14] Still, the idea that the plague was hemorrhoids isn't without precedent. In the Vulgate, St. Jerome's Latin translation of the Bible, he renders it as "swellings of the secret parts," and there *are* times when God threatens hemorrhoids in the Bible—see Deuteronomy 28:27, for instance.[15] In any case, I'd like to make it clear that I'm firmly on the side of the "hemorrhoids" rendering, not because of any linguistic insight I possess but because I prefer whichever version allows me to make more butt jokes.

Anyway, the Philistines proceed to pass the ark around to various cities, but the plague of hemorrhoids, along with a totally adorable plague of mice, follows it wherever it goes. Eventually, they take the hint that the ark is just going to be (wait for it) a big pain in the butt, and they decide to send it back to Israel to make it *their* problem. They don't want to send it back empty-handed,

---

11. Wow, you actually looked at the footnote for that one? Nerd. Briefly, though, "emerod" comes from the Old French word "emoroyde," while the modern word "hemorrhoid" is a direct transliteration of the original Greek word "haimorrhoide."

12. See the ESV, NIV, and NASB translations of this verse, for example.

13. Iqbal Akhtar Khan, "Plague: The Dreadful Visitation Occupying the Human Mind for Centuries," *Transactions of the Royal Society of Tropical Medicine and Hygeine* 98, no. 5 (2004): 270–77.

14. Fred Punzo, *The Biology of Camel Spiders: Arachnida Solifugae* (Berlin: Springer Science & Business Media, 2012), 3.

15. Also see the commentary on this verse in the Babylonian Talmud, *Megillah* 25b.

though, so they consult the priests of Dagon on what would make for an appropriate guilt offering. The priests come up with this charming suggestion:

> **Five golden emerods, and five golden mice.** . . . Wherefore ye shall make images of your emerods, and images of your mice that mar the land; and **ye shall give glory unto the God of Israel.** (1 Samuel 6:4b–5a KJV)

Because what better way to **give glory unto the God of Israel** than with some fourteen-carat anus blossoms? (And they say Philistines don't appreciate art.) I have no idea what a golden representation of a hemorrhoid even looks like, though, seeing as there's not really a standard shape for the things.[16] And now I can't get the image out of my head of some poor, afflicted soul bending over and spreading 'em wide while a lucky Philistine craftsman hammers away at the gold, trying to get the shape *just right*. So, thanks for that, King James.

BEARDS, BUTTS, AND DIPLOMACY

In the tenth chapter of 2 Samuel, King David sends some messengers to Hanun, king of the Ammonites, as a gesture of goodwill, but Hanun isn't having it:

> So Hanun seized David's envoys, shaved off half of each man's beard, **cut off their garments at the buttocks**, and sent them away. (verse 4 NIV)

---

16. Rendering the word as "boil" or "tumor" hardly solves this problem either.

They then limp back to Jericho with their butt cheeks flapping in the breeze.

David helpfully tells the men to hide out at Jericho until their beards regrow. Strangely, though, the Bible never mentions whether he hooks them up with pants, so you can draw your own conclusions about his priorities.

Elijah Thinks Your God Is Pooping

In the eighteenth chapter of 1 Kings, the prophet Elijah finds himself butting[17] heads with the prophets of Baal, an ancient Near Eastern god best known for not actually existing. *They* sure seem to think he's a thing, though, so Elijah proposes a wager: Each team will build an altar and put a sacrifice on it, and then they'll all wait around for their respective deity to set the things ablaze. Whichever one actually shows up for the barbecue is the real one. (It's science!)

Baal's prophets agree to the arrangement, build their altar, and start praying for fire. It goes about as well as you're probably expecting:

> And they took the bull that was given them, and they prepared it and called upon the name of Baal from morning until noon, saying, "O Baal, answer us!" **But there was no voice, and no one answered.** And they limped around the altar that they had made. . . . And they cried aloud and **cut themselves after**

---

17. Heh.

their custom with swords and lances, until the blood gushed out upon them. (verses 26, 28)

I guess their interpretive dance is entertaining for only a few hours, because eventually Elijah gets bored and starts making poop jokes:

And at noon Elijah mocked them, saying, "Cry aloud, for he is a god. Either he is musing, **or he is relieving himself**, or he is on a journey, or perhaps he is asleep and must be awakened." (verse 27)

To **relieve oneself**, I'm sure you're aware, is a fairly common (if stodgy) euphemism for taking a dump. There are plenty of English translations that obscure the meaning here, but the Hebrew verb is *sig*, which literally translates to "pursue" or "step aside," and almost always has a euphemistic connotation, *á la* "see a man about a horse."[18] Elijah's taunt more or less amounts to "Shout louder—he might be in the john," so it's probably good he never quit his prophesying day job for a career in stand-up.

In case you're wondering, Baal never shows up to the party. Midafternoon, once the other prophets are lying around, moaning and delirious from blood loss, Elijah figures it's as good a time as any to build his own altar. He piles up twelve stones, puts a bull and some firewood on top of it, and says,

"Fill four jars with water and pour it on the burnt offering and on the wood." And he said, "Do it a second time." And they did it a second time. And he said, "Do it a third time." And

---

18. Gary A. Rendsburg, "The Mock of Baal in 1 Kings 18:27," *Catholic Biblical Quarterly* 50, no. 3 (1988): 414–17.

they did it a third time. **And the water ran around the altar and filled the trench also with water.** (verses 33b–35)

So not only is he going to make God light up his own altar, but he's going to make it as flame-retardant as possible first, because Elijah doesn't waste time on subtlety. Given the Bible's broadly pro-God stance, though, it's not entirely shocking that God comes through. Elijah says a few words of prayer,

Then **the fire of the LORD fell** and consumed the burnt offering and the wood and the stones and the dust, and licked up the water that was in the trench. And when all the people saw it, they fell on their faces and said, "The LORD, he is God; the LORD, he is God." (verses 38–39)

So God wins one for the proverbial Gipper, and everyone in Israel converts back to the one true faith.

Oh, and Elijah murders every last one of Baal's prophets, because people were *hard-core* in the Old Testament.

WE NEED TO HAVE A SERIOUS CHAT ABOUT HOW FACE-MELTINGLY AWESOME ST. PAUL WAS

In his letter to the Philippians, the apostle Paul lists some of the things he gave up to follow Jesus:

I count all things but loss for the excellency of the knowledge of Christ Jesus my Lord: for whom I have

suffered the loss of all things, and do count them
but **dung**, that I may win Christ. (Philippians 3:8 KJV)

When he says he's "suffered the loss of all things,"
he's not exaggerating too much, seeing as Paul was
famously imprisoned and eventually martyred. On the
upside, though, he says all the cool stuff he used to
have was basically **"dung."**

Except he doesn't actually say **dung**, since the
word in the original Greek is *skubala*, which most
scholars will tell you is a vulgarity roughly equivalent
to "sh*t."[19]

Most modern translations neuter this passage
even more than the King James, rendering *skubala* as
either "rubbish" (ESV) or "garbage" (NIV), which is too
bad, since it sort of obscures what a boss St. Paul was.
The book of Acts portrays him surviving shipwrecks
and shaking off snakebites like some sort of ancient
Samuel L. Jackson, but modern translators won't even
let him drop an *s*-word.

Isaac Meets Rebekah (While Pooping)

One of the Bible's best poop jokes happens fairly early on, in the
book of Genesis, when Abraham decides to find a wife for his
son Isaac. God promised Abraham more descendants than the

---

19. Simon Critchley, "You Are Not Your Own," in *Politics of Religion / Religion
of Politics*, ed. Alistair Welchman (Berlin: Springer, 2014), 11–28.

sand of the shores and the stars of the sky (which is cool, but personally, I would have held out for a pony), so making sure his kid gets married off and makes some babies is kind of a big deal to him. That's probably why the whole thing kicks off with this charming exchange:

> And Abraham said to his servant, the oldest of his household, who had charge of all that he had, "**Put your hand under my thigh**, that I may make you swear by the LORD, the God of heaven and God of the earth, that you will not take a wife for my son from the daughters of the Canaanites, among whom I dwell, but will go to my country and to my kindred, and take a wife for my son Isaac." (Genesis 24:2–4)

Surprisingly, this moment—where Abraham asks his servant to grab his thigh—is actually *not* the butt joke here. In fact, there's a fair amount of consensus among scholars that Abraham is asking his servant to grab his genitals.[20] Abraham is asking him to swear on his crotch, the same way modern people might swear on a Bible.[21]

If that seems weird to you (and I'm not sure why it *would*, but if it *does*), the key here is that the oath the servant is taking is an oath to maintain Abraham's hereditary line. In other words, this is an oath directly related to Abraham's baby-making ability, so he's making this as clear to his servant as possible: "You screw this up, you're not just letting *me* down, you're letting *my balls* down."

---

20. Meir Malul, "More on Pahad Yishāq (Genesis XXXI 42, 53) and the Oath by the Thigh," *Vetus Testamentum* 35, no. 2 (1985): 192–200.

21. The Bible wasn't a thing yet, and you gotta swear on something, right?

So to speak.

I know I promised you butts here,[22] so let's press on.[23] After some ceremonial crotch-grabbing,[24] the servant travels to Abraham's homeland and picks up Isaac's cousin Rebekah, who thinks traveling somewhere she's never been to marry a cousin she's never met sounds like a super idea, and they make their way back toward Abraham's neck of the woods. What follows feels like the prototypical meet-cute:

> And Isaac went out to **meditate** in the field toward evening. And he lifted up his eyes and saw, and behold, there were camels coming. And Rebekah lifted up her eyes, and when she saw Isaac, she **dismounted** from the camel and said to the servant, "Who is that man, walking in the field to meet us?" The servant said, "It is my master." So she took her veil and covered herself. . . . Then Isaac brought her into the tent of Sarah his mother and took Rebekah, and she became his wife, and he loved her. So Isaac was comforted after his mother's death. (verses 63–65, 67)

Aside from that stray bit of Oedipal weirdness at the end, this seems like it could have easily been a scene from a delightful rom-com, possibly starring some combination of Witherspoons and McConaugheys. Except, if you've figured out how this book works by now, you know I'm about to ruin it with butts. Or, more to the point, *improve* it with butts.

---

22. The thigh thing was just too good to ignore, and there wasn't really another place for it. Sorry.

23. Heh.

24. Actually, the text never says the servant obeys Abraham's command to grab his crotch. Maybe he refused. I hope Abraham wasn't weird about it.

Let's start with the first bolded word: **meditate**. The word in the original Hebrew is *lasuah*,[25] which is rendered as "meditate" in most modern English translations only because biblical scholars aren't big on just inserting "[we haven't a clue]" and calling it a day. The word appears nowhere else in Scripture and almost nowhere in other surviving ancient texts, making it difficult to translate,[26] so what we've been left with until recently has been whatever the translator's wildest guess was—everything from "meditate" (NLT) to "stroll" (NET) to "hang his head in shame over his father's habit of making servants grab his junk" (probably).

It was only recently that scholars came across a cognate in Arabic that can be translated, with a fair amount of certainty, as "to dig a pit." And if that sounds weirdly specific, just know that it's pretty much always a euphemism, occasionally for peeing, but usually for pooping.[27] Because all that poop has to go somewhere.

Once you learn *that*, it makes a lot more sense when you find out that the word rendered **"dismounted"** there is actually *naphal*, the Hebrew verb for "to fall."[28] We're not talking about a graceful dismount; we're talking about a woman looking up, seeing a guy too clueless to at least hide in the bushes when he takes a dump, and falling on her butt in the mud—less Nora Ephron, more Three Stooges.

But, as you might have noticed in the last sentence of the passage, Rebekah and Isaac still go through with the marriage. So, hey, happy ending—as long as no one asks how they met, I guess.

---

25. Gary A. Rendsburg, "Lāśûaḥ in Genesis XXIV 63," *Vetus Testamentum* 45, no. 4 (1995): 558–60.

26. Judy Klitsner, *Subversive Sequels in the Bible: How Biblical Stories Mine and Undermine Each Other* (Jerusalem: Koren Publishers, 2011), 166.

27. Rendsburg, "Lāśûaḥ."

28. Some classic translations, like Luther's German Bible, actually preserve this.

GOD IS SUPER SICK OF STEPPING IN YOUR POOP

The overarching narrative of the first five books of the Bible is one of God taking a bunch of recently freed slaves and turning them into a civilized nation, so we shouldn't be surprised that stuff like this keeps popping up in it:

> "You shall have a place outside the camp, and you shall go out to it. And you shall have a trowel with your tools, and when you sit down outside, you shall dig a hole with it and **turn back and cover up your excrement**." (Deuteronomy 23:12–13)

Yep—included in one of the very first sets of laws God gave to the Israelites is "Don't crap in the middle of the camp." And apparently, "Because it's gross" isn't enough of a reason for them either, because God immediately adds this:

> "Because **the LORD your God walks in the midst of your camp**, to deliver you and to give up your enemies before you, therefore your camp must be holy, so that he may not see anything indecent among you and turn away from you." (verse 14)

It's not hard to imagine God thinking about explaining microbes to them before sighing, giving up, and turning into Dustin Hoffman: *Because I'm walkin' here.*

Ehud and the Poopsplosion

But maybe you're not looking for romantic advice from the Bible. Maybe you were hoping for a story about the dangers of stabbing fat people. I can help you there as well!

This one is found in the book of Judges, which, if you're unfamiliar, tells the story of Israel's earliest days in the promised land. There's sort of a cyclical structure to it:

1. Everything is a-okay in Israel.
2. They start worshiping foreign gods, just for fun (after super-extra-pinky-swearing they wouldn't).
3. God allows a foreign power to conquer them as punishment.
4. They admit idol worship wasn't the best idea and ask God to save them.
5. God raises up a so-called judge (which, in this context, means a military leader) to save them.
6. The judge saves them.
7. Everyone goes back to worshiping idols, like, five minutes later.

This all happens a dozen or so times in the book, which includes famous Sunday school–ready stories like Gideon and Samson. On the other hand, it also includes the story of Ehud, which you won't be learning from a Sunday school teacher anytime soon.

In this particular story, it's the Moabites who have conquered and enslaved Israel. After eighteen years of paying exorbitant tribute to Moab's king, Eglon, Israel decides their situation sucks and cries out to God to deliver them. God says, "Ugh, fine," and raises up Ehud, described in the text as "a left-handed man." That detail might not seem important, but it's a thing. Here's why:

> The people of Israel sent tribute by him to Eglon the king of Moab. And Ehud made for himself a sword with two edges, a cubit in length, and **he bound it on his right thigh** under his clothes. And he presented the tribute to Eglon king of Moab. (Judges 3:15b–17a)

The text doesn't say it explicitly, because it assumes a basic knowledge of swordsmanship on the part of the reader (what, you don't have that?), but the gist here is as follows: (1) Most people who have swords sheathe them on the hip opposite their dominant hand, because it's easier to draw them that way. (2) Since most people are right-handed, most people sheathe their sword on their left hip. (3) Eglon's guards would have naturally searched Ehud for weapons, but since they usually dealt with righties, they apparently didn't bother to check both of his hips.[29] (4) Feel free to insert your own TSA joke here.

Also, there's this:

> Now Eglon was **a very fat man.** (verse 17b)

Like the left-handed thing, that bit of body-shaming might not seem important, but it will come into play in a minute.

Ehud presents his tribute, and then he tells Eglon he also has a message for him that he can only deliver in private. Eglon says

---

29. This is doubly tragic when you consider that hips don't lie.

something along the lines of "Mm-hmm, yes, that sounds like a very legitimate, nonsuspicious thing, and you are definitely not trying to murder and/or proposition me," and then:

> And Ehud came to him as he was sitting alone in his cool roof chamber. And Ehud said, "I have a message from God for you." And he arose from his seat. And Ehud reached with his left hand, **took the sword from his right thigh, and thrust it into his belly**. (verses 20–21)

And before you can say, "How in the world did someone as naïvely trusting as Eglon ever become king in the first place?" things go from bad to worse:

> And the hilt also went in after the blade, and the fat closed over the blade, for he did not pull the sword out of his belly; **and the dung came out.** (verse 22)

Ehud can't be bothered to pull his sword out, and **the fat closes over the blade**. Does that even make sense, anatomically? Does fat even work that way? *Do the laws of physics work that way?*[30] Oh, and when the fat closes over the blade, **the dung comes out**. So if you stab a sufficiently overweight person in the belly, his belly will swallow the blade and he'll explode in a shower of poop. Now you know!

Ehud escapes by essentially climbing out the window:

> Then Ehud went out into the porch and **closed the doors of the roof chamber** behind him and locked them. (verse 23)

---

30. Maybe the Bible takes place inside an *Itchy & Scratchy* cartoon?

You'd think it would be only a matter of minutes before Eglon's guards find out what happened, chase Ehud down, and kill him where he stands, but you'd be wrong:

> When he had gone, the servants came, and when they saw that the doors of the roof chamber were locked, they thought, **"Surely he is relieving himself** in the closet of the cool chamber." And **they waited till they were embarrassed**. (verses 24–25a)

When the guards hear the grunting and straining and smell the aroma of a dairy farm in the air, they just shrug and say, "Ugh, he's taking one of his monster dumps again," and then waste countless hours arguing over who has to empty the chamber pot *this* time. Meanwhile, Ehud has plenty of time to escape, go home, raise up an army, and banish the Moabites from Israel for a solid eighty years. Because when God is on your side, you'll always smell the sweet scent of victory, which just happens to smell very similar to the scent of an overweight monarch literally pooping his guts out.

CHAPTER TWO

THERE IS NO COMMANDMENT TO WEAR PANTS

Nudity, Much of It Gratuitous

Humanity and nudity have a complicated relationship. Studies show many of us are born naked,[citation needed] but most of us put on clothes pretty soon thereafter and take them off fairly rarely for the rest of our lives—mainly for bathing, sex, and when we need to count to eleven. The rest of the time, most cultures encourage the wearing of clothing, although the amount of clothing and the extent to which it's encouraged varies. There are civilizations who mercilessly punish anyone who dares to show his or her (but let's be honest: her) ankles, and there are cultures who think *you're* the weird one if you won't strip down for their mixed-gender saunas.

So we're all hung up on nudity in different ways, but the common thread (if you will) seems to be that we *are* all hung up on it. The Bible has at least something of an explanation for this—there was some fruit and a talking snake involved, which, as any New Atheist will tell you, is *obviously just ridiculous*, and also they're the first person in history to notice that talking snakes are not universal to the human experience. If you buy into the story, though, you know that being hung up on nudity is a metaphor for shame, or a literal effect of it, or both, or whatever. However you want to take it, though, the point is hard to argue with: like the fish who finally learned what water was, ever since we noticed we were naked, we've thought that nudity was a *super* big deal.

Whether nudity is awesome or just the worst, though, is something people have differed on over the years, with the main consideration being how attractive the nude person was. You see this reflected in Scripture, where the nudity ebbs and flows as the culture changes around it. Sometimes it's portrayed as basically okay, sometimes it's portrayed as shameful, and sometimes it's contentious even within the passage itself, but one thing remains constant: it's *always* hilarious.

Depending, of course, on what you find funny.

Noah Was Basically a Moonshining Hillbilly

Like the book of Judges, the book of Genesis can more or less be divided roughly in half: about half the material seems tailor-made for Sunday school classes, while the other half would make an HBO producer blush—and the Noah's ark narrative is perhaps the poster child for this. On the surface, it might seem like something dreamed up by a marketing team to sell church nursery décor, but it's got a dark subtext (really, a dark *text*): everyone on earth, except for eight people, gets brutally murdered by God. It's like one of those Marvel movies where they level New York City for the umpteenth time—some innocent fun, unless you think about it for more than two seconds.

Still, the basic thrust[1] of the narrative is one of hope: even if the proliferation of evil leads God to destroy the world, he still saves a handful of virtuous, upstanding people so that the human race and creation can flourish in the future—this time without the evil part. Right? Yay, evil-free world! Maybe even without exposed butts!

Except, never mind.

Because even the best people are still basically awful, it takes Noah all of five minutes after docking the ark to do something insane and embarrassing. In his case, that means planting a vineyard, making some bathtub wine, and getting falling-down drunk:

> Noah began to be a man of the soil, and he planted a vineyard. He drank of the wine and **became drunk and lay uncovered in his tent**. (Genesis 9:20–21)

I think there's a lesson to be learned here, and it's that seeing stuff will *mess you up*, man. Noah wasn't just a sweet old guy who loved God and then got to cuddle with some lions and giraffes for a couple of months; he was someone who had *literally witnessed the apocalypse*. You don't watch nearly everyone you know die horrible, violent deaths (drowned, dashed on rocks, eaten by very happy sharks, etc.) and not come out on the other side at least a little bit shell-shocked. We all have something we turn to to dull the pain; in Noah's case, it was moonshining.

But then things get weirder:

---

1. Heh.

And Ham, the father of Canaan, **saw the nakedness of his father** and told his two brothers outside. (verse 22)

Ham, by the way, is Noah's youngest son[2]—and he's apparently so fascinated by the sight of his father's drunk, naked butt that he can't keep the news to himself. "Ever wanted to see Dad's penis? Now's your chance, guys!" That pitch fails to stir the souls of Shem and Japheth, however, who decide to protect Dad's dignity (such as it is):

> Then Shem and Japheth took a garment, laid it on both their shoulders, and walked backward and covered the nakedness of their father. **Their faces were turned backward**, and they did not see their father's nakedness. (verse 23)

When Noah wakes up, he is *not* happy:

> When Noah awoke from his wine and knew what his youngest son had done to him, he said, "**Cursed be Canaan**; a servant of servants shall he be to his brothers." He also said, "**Blessed be the LORD, the God of Shem**; and let Canaan be his servant. **May God enlarge Japheth,**[3] and let him dwell in the tents of Shem, and let Canaan be his servant." (verses 24–27)

---

2. Weirdly, the Bible places these events in the vicinity of Mount Ararat, which is located in modern-day Turkey. So Noah named his son Ham and settled in Turkey, because the last ten thousand years of history were secretly just setting me up for a club sandwich joke.

3. Heh. (For what it's worth, this is actually a pun in the original Hebrew. Since puns are never funny, and they're especially unfunny when you try to translate them, I'll let you look it up for yourself.)

Canaan is Ham's son, by the way, if that makes this passage a bit clearer, which it probably doesn't. Apparently, just because Ham saw his doodle, Noah feels entitled to curse Ham's children, and his children's children, and his children's children's children, because that was just how they did things in the Old Testament.[4] That probably seems a little harsh, which is where some of the more out-there interpretations of this passage come from—like, maybe, according to certain commentators, Ham slipped Noah a *big slice of Ham*, if you know what I mean. Or possibly took a slice off of *Noah's* ham.

What I'm trying to say is that a common interpretation of this passage is that Ham either sodomized or castrated Noah, or possibly both. I'm not saying this just for shock value, nor am I quoting some random modern-day speculation. These ideas come straight from the Babylonian Talmud—one of the ancient, foundational texts to modern Judaism—which contains a brief discourse between two rabbis, one of whom favors the castration theory and the other of whom favors anal rape. (I mean he favors the theory, not that he . . . never mind. You get it.)[5] And while, yes, either one of those two acts would justify Noah's curse a bit more, it's not entirely clear *why* Ham would be interested in performing either act. I guess when your dad traps you on a boat that reeks of poop for months on end, it inevitably changes how you feel about him.

One way or another.

I should probably also address the so-called Curse of Ham here, since it's got an ugly recent history in the West. In

---

4. It was particularly popular directly after the Flood, seeing as there was a severe shortage of currently alive people to curse.
5. Babylonian Talmud, Sanhedrin 70a.

the context of the passage, it's pretty clear it's there to cast the Canaanites in a negative light and justify Israel's conquest of the Holy Land.[6] But at some point in the last few centuries, many white Christians latched on to the idea that the curse consisted of dark skin,[7] so in their minds that somehow made it a-okay to enslave people of African descent.[8] The fact that no one figured out this interpretation until enslaving black people had already become globally popular probably should have given them pause, but then again, plenty of Christians are good at nothing if not taking random scriptural texts out of context to justify whatever they're already doing.

BOTCH AN EXORCISM, END UP NAKED

You don't have to go to the cineplex to see a hilarious botch-job of an exorcism; just crack open a New Testament. In the nineteenth chapter of Acts, when Christianity is starting to get big and exorcisms are all the rage, some aspiring cool kids tell a demon, "I adjure you by the Jesus whom Paul proclaims," and the demon . . . does this:

---

6. Robert Alter, *The Five Books of Moses: A Translation with Commentary* (New York: W.W. Norton & Company, 2008), 52.

7. To be 100 percent clear, Noah doesn't say anything at all about dark skin in the curse. This interpretation turns entirely on the fact that the word "Ham" sounds somewhat similar to an etymologically unrelated word for "dark." Eisegetes are weird.

8. Edith R. Sanders, "The Hamitic Hypothesis; Its Origins and Functions in Time Perspective," *Journal of African History* 10, no. 4 (1969): 521–32.

> But the evil spirit answered them, **"Jesus I know, and Paul I recognize, but who are you?"** And the man in whom was the evil spirit leaped on them, mastered all of them and overpowered them, so that **they fled out of that house naked and wounded**. (verses 15–16)
>
> Demons, in other words, aren't content just to spin people's heads around and make them puke pea soup—they will also cheerfully strip you naked.

Is Saul Among the Prophets? Yes. The Naked Prophets.

For Noah, nudity was a big taboo. There are other moments in the Bible, though, where nudity appears to be accepted, or even expected. In Saul and David's time, for instance, prophets were apparently supposed to be naked. Like, just all the time. It was a thing.

I addressed Saul and David's bizarre relationship in the previous chapter, but since I know you skimmed it, here's a quick recap: Saul is king over Israel. He also likes to fly into murderous rages. He *also* strongly suspects David is trying to usurp his throne. Hey, why not combine those two interests? So he spends the better part of 1 Samuel trying to hunt David down.

In this particular instance, David has just married Saul's daughter Michal, but Saul barely lets them get through the honeymoon before he starts sending armed guards to bang on their door. When they show up, Michal sends David out the back window, and:

Michal **took the household idol** and laid it on the bed, and put a quilt of goats' hair at its head, and covered it with clothes. When Saul sent messengers to take David, she said, "He is sick." (1 Samuel 19:13–14 NASB)

As a side note here, the internet often seems to be crawling with unreasonably angry atheists pointing to archeological finds of idols in the Holy Land as evidence that the Bible isn't true. This would be entirely reasonable, except the Old Testament itself portrays ancient Israel as a place where literally everyone, including one of its most revered figures, had houses stuffed full of idols, some of which were occasionally given stylish goat-hair wigs for the purposes of Ferris Bueller-esque hijinks.

Anyway, David escapes to a place called "Naioth in Ramah," where the prophet Samuel is hanging out with all the other prophets of Israel. It's like a big prophecy convention. When Saul figures out Michal's ruse, he sends some more guards to Naioth, where this happens:

Then Saul sent messengers to take David, and when they saw the company of the prophets prophesying, and Samuel standing as head over them, **the Spirit of God came upon the messengers of Saul, and they also prophesied.** (verse 20)

Apparently the spirit of prophesying is just too much for these guys, so they start prophesying and forget entirely to grab David. If there's a lesson for Saul here, it's that you probably shouldn't send other people to do your dirty work for you:

> When it was told Saul, he sent other messengers, and they also prophesied. (verse 21a)

Some people have to learn the hard way, though.

> And Saul sent messengers again the third time, and they also prophesied. (verse 21b)

The *really* hard way.

There's an old saying that the definition of insanity is doing the same thing again and again, expecting different results. Personally, I'd think a better definition for insanity would be "repeatedly flying into a murderous rage and trying to kill your court musician / son-in-law." But either way, Saul qualifies.

I promised you nudity, though, so let me cut to the chase. It's around this time that Saul finally comes to his senses (such as they are) and goes to kill David himself:

> And he went there to Naioth in Ramah. **And the Spirit of God came upon him also**, and as he went **he prophesied** until he came to Naioth in Ramah. (verse 23)

The pull of the big prophecy rave is so strong that Saul himself can't resist it, and he joins in even before he gets there. Then, apropos of nothing, the author of 1 Samuel adds this note:

> **And he too stripped off his clothes**, and he too prophesied before Samuel **and lay naked** all that day and all that night. (verse 24a)

So, evidently, for the author of 1 Samuel, it's such a normal thing to get naked while you're prophesying that he feels no need to explain it. Just, "Yup, he was prophesying. Stripped naked and everything."

If stripping naked to prophesy seems strange, just know that this isn't even the only time it happens in the Bible. About a thousand pages and three hundred years later, we get this:

> At that time the LORD spoke by Isaiah the son of Amoz, saying, "Go, and loose the sackcloth from your waist and take off your sandals from your feet," **and he did so, walking naked and barefoot**. (Isaiah 20:2)

In Isaiah's case, it's not that he's just overcome with the spirit of the moment; God literally comes to him and says, "Hey, time to prophesy! You know what that means! Strip!" In *this* particular context, though, the nudity is at least an object lesson for the ravages of war:

> Then the LORD said, "As my servant Isaiah has walked naked and barefoot for three years as a sign and a portent against Egypt and Cush, so shall the king of Assyria lead away the Egyptian captives and the Cushite exiles, both the young and the old, naked and barefoot, **with buttocks uncovered**, the nakedness of Egypt." (verses 3–4)

. . . whereas, Saul **uncovered his buttocks** for seemingly no reason at all. But I guess that's the difference between the Old Testament's greatest major prophet and its biggest hack of a king: a basic appreciation for symbolism.

ON THE WRONG WAY TO GET YOUR NEIGHBOR NAKED

Railing against the evils of the Neo-Babylonian Empire, the prophet Habakkuk writes:

"Woe to him who makes his neighbors drink—

you pour out your wrath and make them drunk,

in order to gaze at their nakedness!" (Habakkuk 2:15)

So, God hates strip poker (or, more to the point, sexual abuse). Now you know.

Ruth Lands Herself a Man

Tucked in behind all the murder and mayhem of Judges (in the Christian Bible, anyway[9]) is the book of Ruth, which is about as close to a sweet little rom-com as anything in the Bible ever gets. Sure, there aren't any Sara Bareilles songs, and the whole thing kicks off with a bunch of starvation and death, but overall, as far as the Old Testament goes, the book is pretty sunny.

It starts out with a massive famine in the Israelite city of Bethlehem, which leaves a guy named Elimelech and his wife, Naomi, starving and desperate. Their solution is to immigrate to Moab, with whom Israel has a bit of a fraught relationship, due mainly to Moab's

---

9. In the Jewish Tanakh, Ruth comes later and actually has something of a special status—together with Song of Songs, Lamentations, Ecclesiastes, and Esther, it's considered one of the Megilloth ("Rolls"), a set of five books that traditionally form the core of annual liturgical readings in many synagogues.

habit of conquering and enslaving them.[10] They hang out there a decade or so, and their two sons marry Moabite women; unfortunately, the famine they were running from eventually reaches Moab as well, and Naomi's husband and sons all end up starving to death. Naomi says, "Welp, I'm obviously poison or something," and decides to head back to Israel, telling her daughters-in-law to stay there and find themselves some nice Moabite husbands who won't die on them. One of them, Ruth, refuses:

> But Ruth said, "Do not urge me to leave you or to return from following you. For where you go I will go, and where you lodge I will lodge. **Your people shall be my people, and your God my God.** Where you die I will die, and there will I be buried. May the LORD do so to me and more also if anything but death parts me from you." (Ruth 1:16–17)

Naomi mutters, "Geez, my son said you were clingy, but I thought he was just venting,"[11] and the two of them head back to Bethlehem together, possibly in a wacky, camel-based road trip montage set to a jaunty Kenny Loggins tune. When they arrive, they settle in for a fun couple of years of slowly starving to death, seeing as the options for women in the ancient Near East were either (1) get married and make babies or (2) starve to death, and they've already both blown it on option number one.

Actually, though, there *is* one other option—albeit a long shot. Hebrew tradition provided for what was called a *goel*, or in some (awkward) English Bible translations, a "kinsman-redeemer."

---

10. See "Ehud and the Poopsplosion," previous chapter.
11. Probably.

The *goel* was whoever happened to be the closest male relative of anyone in serious economic trouble, and he would have several duties, including marrying and impregnating a woman who had been left widowed and childless.[12] Creepy and vaguely incestuous, sure, but it kept people from starving. (Usually. Sometimes.)

So if Ruth *doesn't* feel like starving, the way forward is clear: find her *goel*.[13] Unfortunately for her, there aren't a lot of close male relatives around (seeing as she's miles from home and her husband, father-in-law, and brother-in-law have all died). Fortunately, Naomi remembers a guy named Boaz, a distant relative of her husband who's also a wealthy farmer ("wealthy farmer" used to be a thing, I promise), and she sends Ruth to "glean" in his fields, *if you know what I mean.* (I mean the ancient Near Eastern practice of collecting crops accidentally dropped by harvesters. It was, in other words, an alternative to begging.) Boaz responds positively, even inviting her to share lunch with the workers and instructing them to deliberately drop extra grain for her.

This is going pretty well, thinks Naomi. *Let's take it to the next level*:

> "Is not Boaz our relative, with whose young women you were?
> See, **he is winnowing barley tonight at the threshing floor.**
> Wash therefore and anoint yourself, and put on your cloak
> and go down to the threshing floor, but do not make yourself
> known to the man until he has finished eating and drinking.
> But when he lies down, observe the place where he lies. Then

---

12. Lesila Raitiqa, "Ruth, Redeemer of the Land," in *Weavings: Women Doing Theology in Oceania*, ed. Lydia Johnson (Suva: University of the South Pacific, 2003), 99–106.

13. It's important to have *goel*s in life. Am I right, folks? I'll see myself out.

go and **uncover his feet** and lie down, and he will tell you what to do." (Ruth 3:2–4)

There's a lot going on here, so let's take a sec to unpack it all. Naomi tells Ruth to clean herself up and throw on some fragrance, which makes sense. Then she tells her to go to his workplace and, um, hide, which—now we're getting into single-camera sitcom territory. Then she tells her *to watch him while he sleeps*, so, yeah, this is all totally normal.

The next step is lie down at his feet, which in the ancient Near East was a fairly universal gesture of submission. Then she **"uncovers his feet."** There are a couple of possibilities for what that might mean, though.

First of all, there's the "innocent" interpretation (which, for the purposes of this book, is also the "wrong" interpretation)—namely that Ruth was uncovering Boaz's feet to invoke the traditional *goel*-binding ritual, in which the woman would remove one of the man's shoes. (Removing shoes was a gesture roughly equivalent to shaking hands at the time.) Under that understanding, Ruth is merely making it clear to Boaz that he's under a legal obligation.

And then, of course, there's the *fun* interpretation.

I touched on this[14] in the previous chapter, but ancient Hebrew frequently uses the word "feet" as a euphemism for genitalia.[15] For that reason, there's at least a handful of commentators who have argued that the book is being coy about what actually transpires between Ruth and Boaz here. It's entirely possible that Naomi is

---

14. Heh.
15. Paul Haupt, "Abraham's Bosom," *American Journal of Philology* 42, no. 2 (1921): 162–67.

sending Ruth on a seduction mission, in order to guilt Boaz into making her an honest woman.[16] Many others have pointed out that such an interpretation goes against the main thrust[17] of the book, which portrays Ruth and Boaz as pious, faithful types, but even the best of us have made regrettable decisions when we woke up half-naked on threshing floors, right?

Right?

In any case, Boaz steps up as Ruth's *goel*, so seduction or not, Naomi's plan works out. So it's either one of those sweet, family-friendly rom-coms they show on the Hallmark Channel, or else it's one of those PG-13 numbers where the protagonists sleep together halfway through, then fight and break up, and then get back together for the end credits, and also there's Hugh Grant or something. Take your pick.

Bible interpretation is fun!

QUEEN VASHTI HAD MANY EMBARRASSING PERSONAL PROBLEMS

In the book of Esther, the Persian emperor divorces his queen after she fails to show up for the party he holds so that his drinking buddies can all see how hot she is:

On the seventh day, when the heart of the king was merry with wine, he commanded ... the seven eunuchs who served in the presence of King Ahasuerus, to

---

16. Thomas W. Mann, "Ruth 4," *Interpretation: A Journal of Bible and Theology* 64, no. 2 (2010): 178–80.

17. Heh.

> bring Queen Vashti before the king with her royal crown, in order **to show the peoples and the princes her beauty**, for she was lovely to look at. **But Queen Vashti refused** to come at the king's command delivered by the eunuchs. (Esther 1:10–12a)

If it seems a little strange that Vashti considered "just show up for the party" to be an unreasonable request, know that, according to several ancient commentaries, Ahasuerus asked her to show up naked.[18] And if that's not salacious enough for you, others insist her refusal wasn't about modesty so much as embarrassment—different accounts claim she either suffered from leprosy or *was given a penis* by the angel Gabriel.[19] No matter how weird the Bible gets, the supplementary material is always weirder.

St. Mark Goes Streaking

Certain scholars—the kind that usually get called "modernist" or "liberal"—argue that most of the books of the New Testament were written a lot later than Christians have historically believed (as much as three or four generations after the life of Christ), and most of them were falsely attributed to their alleged authors long after the fact, in an attempt to grant them credibility. I'm

---

18. Yalkut Shimoni Esther 1049, Esther Rabbah 4, Pirke De-Rabbi Eliezer 48.
19. Eliezer Segal, *Holidays, History, and Halakhah* (Lanham, MD: Jason Aronson, Inc., 2001), 126.

not a Bible scholar, but I always found that premise a bit odd. If ancient Christians were really trying to grant the Gospels credibility-by-association, why are three of them attributed to relative nobodies? You probably know who John was (he's got four other New Testament books credited to him), but who in the world were Matthew, Mark, and Luke?

Maybe you remember Matthew was one of the apostles, but do you have any idea what he did as an apostle, besides write his namesake book? (If you're going to falsely attribute a gospel to an apostle, why not Peter or James?) That leaves Mark and Luke, who are both known for writing *their* gospels, and—aside from following Peter and Paul (respectively) around like lost puppies—not much else. Luke wrote Acts, so that's *something*, I guess; Mark . . . founded the church in Alexandria? That's not *nothing*, but I doubt you'll see it on a Trivial Pursuit card.

What you *might* see on a Trivial Pursuit card, though, is that Mark ran around naked the night Jesus was arrested. (Possibly.)

So, real quick, who was Mark? Also known as "John Mark" (twice the names, for twice the fun), he was an early follower of Jesus and possibly one of the "seventy disciples" referred to in Luke 10. After Jesus' death, he followed Peter around on his missionary journeys and apparently took copious notes, since most of the gospel of Mark is traditionally thought to be derived from Peter's sermons (treating them as sort of an oral "sayings" tradition).[20] But then, he would have also witnessed some of

---

20. In William L. Lane's commentary on Mark's gospel, he points out that the book as a whole seems to draw even its basic outline from the sermon Peter preaches in Acts 10.

the events himself. And he would have witnessed some of them naked.

I've been promising you nudity for several paragraphs now,[21] so let me cut to the literal chase. Mark's gospel ends more or less the same way the other three do, with Jesus' Last Supper, arrest, trial, and crucifixion.[22] So Jesus and his disciples share a meal, they relax in the garden, Judas shows up and pulls a Judas, Jesus is arrested, and all his friends scatter. Including . . . this guy:

> And a young man followed him, with nothing but a linen cloth about his body. And they seized him, but he left the linen cloth and **ran away naked**. (Mark 14:51–52)

So the guards who come to arrest Jesus are so into arresting people that they're basically just grabbing everyone they see, including this half-dressed kid who happens to be around, and he's so not into getting arrested that he runs off *au naturel*. This is the last verse of the arrest narrative, by the way—"Oh yeah, and some kid ran away naked." Maybe that seems anti-climactic, but scholars of ancient literature will tell you that the anonymity of the young man strongly suggests the note is an autobiographical one[23]—meaning that, since this is the only

---

21. This is how all the great writers do it, by the way. People will keep turning pages as long as they think something steamy is just seconds away. The other Great Writer Secret™, in case you were wondering, is to think up endless synonyms for "turgid manhood."

22. Curiously, it omits a resurrection narrative, at least in the earliest manuscripts we have. The Bible is weird.

23. Tom Wright, *Mark for Everyone* (Louisville, KY: Westminster John Knox Press, 2001), 200.

time Mark inserted himself into his own gospel,[24] he apparently thought it was *very* important that you, the reader, knew about that time he ran through the Garden of Gethsemane naked.

In case you're wondering, no, it's not *that* weird that the young man is wearing "nothing but a linen cloth." It was basically an undergarment, but not a particularly indecent one—more or less the ancient Near Eastern equivalent of walking to the mailbox in jorts and Crocs. Awkward and casual, but not *that* unusual. In any case, it's hard to say why Mark felt compelled to include this particular detail, unless it's just a way of underlining the previous verse:

And they **all left him** and fled. (verse 50)

In other words, Mark wants to be sure you know that *everybody* abandoned Jesus the night he was arrested—his cynical hangers-on, his most devoted followers, even that kid who was always tagging along in his underwear.[25] Alternatively, it might just be a subtle signature on the manuscript, or possibly an injoke for the people of the early church. Which means, in a way, I'm carrying on an important tradition here.

[*High-fives self.*]

---

24. Actually, the "Secret Gospel of Mark"—a lost document we now know about only from a letter allegedly written by St. Clement of Alexandria in the first century—contains additional stories about the young man in linen. But that complicates things, and scholars can't even agree on whether Clement's letter, let alone the "Secret Gospel," are legit. So who knows.

25. To spell it out even further, the apparent subtext is that, if you're thinking, "Well, *I* wouldn't have left Jesus," you're probably wrong.

ST. PETER DRESSED FOR THE JOB HE WANTED

In the last few chapters of the gospel of John, the newly resurrected Christ appears multiple times to his disciples and followers. In chapter 21, he shows up on the shore while Peter is out in his fishing boat:

> When Simon Peter heard that it was the Lord, he put on his outer garment, **for he was stripped for work**, and threw himself into the sea. (John 21:7b)

And now you know that Peter went fishing naked. Or at least partially naked. He was living the dream.

David Dances Naked

Remember earlier in this chapter, when I mentioned that David married Saul's daughter Michal, and then Saul tried to kill him yet again (that wacky Saul), and Michal had to buy David some time by putting an idol and some goat's hair in the bed? Cute story (sort of), but it turns out that, while marrying the daughter of the king whose throne you're eyeing might be great for your political ambitions, it doesn't necessarily lead to marital bliss. What I'm trying to say is, David and Michal's marriage isn't all hide-the-hairy-idol-in-the-bed.

Things start to get really sour around the time David becomes king over Israel and consolidates his power further by bringing the ark of the covenant to his capital city of Jerusalem. It's been a long time since anyone in Jerusalem has laid eyes on the sacred golden box, so David gets pretty excited when it rolls up:

> And David **danced before the LORD** with all his might. And David was **wearing a linen ephod**. (2 Samuel 6:14)

Modern scholars aren't entirely sure what an **ephod** was, but we *do* know that it was a priestly garment, so, as a nonpriest, David wasn't supposed to be wearing it. It also wasn't an entire set of clothes, so David appears to have been, at best, half-dressed here,[26] which makes sense, since, as *Risky Business* taught us, the only correct way to celebrate anything is to dance around in your Underoos. But regardless of the exact nature of the garment, it sure seems to bother Michal:

> Michal the daughter of Saul looked out of the window and saw King David leaping and dancing before the LORD, and **she despised him in her heart**. (verse 16b)

People disagree about what exactly sets Michal off here. Modern commentators tend to focus on the class aspects of the dance—that is, the king of Israel shouldn't have been dressing like a priest or dancing like a commoner.[27] Michal, on the other hand, puts it another way:

---

26. N. L. Tidwell, "The Linen Ephod: 1 Sam. II 18 and 2 Sam. VI 14," *Vetus Testamentum* 24, no. 4 (1974): 505–7.

27. David J. A. Clines, "Michal Observed: An Introduction to Reading Her Story," in *Telling Queen Michal's Story: An Experiment in Comparative Interpretation*, ed. David J. A. Clines and Tamara C. Eskenazi (Sheffield: Sheffield Academic Press, 1991), 24–63.

But Michal the daughter of Saul came out to meet David and said, "How the king of Israel honored himself today, **uncovering himself** today before the eyes of his servants' female servants, as one of the vulgar fellows **shamelessly uncovers himself!**" (verse 20b)

Outrage over "decency" can frequently be a thin disguise for classism, but taken at face value, Michal appears to believe that David has given their female servants the full monty. (And she might be right—the medieval rabbi Rashi argues that the ephod consisted of, at most, an apron.[28]) But in any case—nude, partially nude, or never-nude—David's response is that Michal needs to relax. After all, the servant girls were really into it.

No, that's actually what he says:

"I will make myself yet more contemptible than this, and I will be abased in your eyes. But **by the female servants of whom you have spoken, by them I shall be held in honor.**" (verse 22)

Because David is the man of the people—more interested in the esteem of God and servants than nobility.

That, or he just really likes to dance naked.

Or both. Let's go with both.

---

28. Theodore Clinton Foote, *The Ephod: Its Form and Use* (Baltimore, MD: Johns Hopkins University, 1902), 38.

THERE IS NO COMMANDMENT TO WEAR PANTS

IN WHICH A WOMAN IS LITERALLY OBJECTIFIED

In the first chapter of 1 Kings, King David (yeah, that guy again) is getting on in years and feeling under the weather:

> Now King David was old and advanced in years. And although they covered him with clothes, he could not get warm. Therefore his servants said to him, "**Let a young woman be sought** for my lord the king, and let her wait on the king and be in his service. **Let her lie in your arms, that my lord the king may be warm.**" (verses 1–2)

The passage goes on to specify that David "knew her not," so apparently David had some sort of Gandhi thing going on, but it's a little weird to think the go-to cure for chronic chilliness was a young woman. I'm almost positive that's not what "hot girl" actually means.

Apparently, If You're a Good Enough Stripper, It's Really Easy to Get Someone Beheaded

Dancing naked isn't *inherently* populist, though. Nor (surprise!) is it always a way to show off your religious piety. Sometimes it's a way to ingratiate yourself with corrupt royalty and get prophets killed—especially if you're female. So yeah, the double standard is alive and well here, but I'm honestly not sure which gender got the short end of the stick on this one.

In the fourteenth chapter of Matthew's gospel, we find the story of John the Baptist's death—you remember John the Baptist, right? The guy who baptized Jesus, along with basically everyone else he met (hence the nickname)? He didn't disappear after Jesus' baptism; he just kept doing what prophets do—he wandered around in a loincloth yelling about how sinful everyone was. As you can imagine, people didn't react super positively to that, especially the people in charge:

> Herod had **seized John and bound him and put him in prison** for the sake of Herodias, his brother Philip's wife, because John had been saying to him, "It is not lawful for you to have her." (verses 3b–4)

King Herod Antipas of Galilee had stolen his brother's wife, and John had pointed out that the king's actions were unethical (and specifically banned in Leviticus 18:16). That made Herod feel bad, so he had thrown John in prison, and now you know politicians haven't changed much in the last two thousand years. He probably would have just left it at that, but then this happens:

> But when Herod's birthday came, **the daughter of Herodias danced before the company and pleased Herod**, so that he promised with an oath to give her whatever she might ask. (verses 6–7)

So, his stepdaughter/niece dances for the court, and she dances so well that he promises her literally whatever she wants (because there is no way *that* promise could go sideways on him). This turns out to be bad news for John:

Prompted by her mother, she said, **"Give me the head of John the Baptist here on a platter."** And the king was sorry, but because of his oaths and his guests he commanded it to be given. He sent and had John beheaded in the prison, and his head was brought on a platter and given to the girl, and she brought it to her mother. (verses 8–11)

It's that "on a platter" detail that pushes this passage over the top—she doesn't just want his head; she wants it on dinnerware. (I personally would have asked for it mounted on a custom bobble-head, but that's just me.) Herod's readiness to comply with such a grisly request has led to endless speculation about the exact nature of his stepdaughter's dance—we know nothing about it from the passage, and the only other ancient source on the dancer is the historian Josephus, who tells us the dancer's name is Salome, and not much else.[29] For all we know, she was dancing the Chicken Dance.[30]

I can hear some of you already: "What about the *Dance of the Seven Veils!?* Everyone knows that *Salome danced the Dance of the Seven Veils!*" Are you ready to be disappointed? Good.

It turns out that the phrase "Dance of the Seven Veils" comes not from history or even ancient tradition, but rather from the nineteenth-century play *Salomé*, written by Oscar Wilde.[31] The dance isn't even described in the script; all it says is "Salomé dances the dance of the seven veils." Presumably, the dance is intended to be sexy—that's how most directors of the play (and the Strauss

---

29. Josephus, *Antiquities of the Jews*, 18.5.4.
30. You may be interested to know that I actually once won a Chicken Dance competition at a roller-skating rink. My life has been downhill ever since.
31. Toni Bentley, *Sisters of Salome* (Lincoln, NE: University of Nebraska Press, 2005), 30.

opera it inspired) have staged it—and Wilde himself seems to have been influenced by the contemporary popularity of "veil dances," which were something Victorian-era Brits thought Middle Eastern women did.[32] As with most things Westerners thought in the nineteenth century, though, this appears to have been entirely a product of their imaginations, which were big on exoticizing and sexualizing everyone who lived anywhere warmer than Norway. So the idea that Salome threw off seven veils, or whatever, was implanted in your head not by the Bible or Christian tradition but by that sarcastic fop who wrote *The Importance of Being Earnest*.

Weirder still, while *Salomé* was far from a popular play—a lot of countries outright banned it for salaciousness—it's been suggested that Wilde inadvertently *invented* the striptease when he wrote it.[33] While sexy dances have presumably always existed, the idea of dancing while throwing off articles of clothing seems to have been relatively unheard of, at least in the West, prior to the publication of *Salomé*. In other words, Oscar Wilde—who, as a gay man, presumably wouldn't have been all that interested in watching a woman strip—wrote a play that expanded a single, relatively innocent sentence in Matthew into the prototypical striptease, which then gave birth to a million burlesque shows, gentlemen's clubs, and PornHub videos.

All that based on a few words from a passage that was supposed to be about an innocent man getting beheaded—because if there's one thing people have always excelled at, it's completely missing the point.

32. Rhonda Garelick, "Electric Salome: Loie Fuller at the Exposition Universelle of 1900," in *Imperialism and Theater: Essays on World Theater, Drama and Performance 1795–1995*, ed. J. Ellen Gainor (New York: Routledge, 1995), 83–100.
33. Bentley, *Sisters of Salome*, 31.

CHAPTER THREE

ALL RIGHT, LET'S GET STARTED ON THE SEX STUFF

There Is a Lot of It

There's a perception among certain people that the Abrahamic tradition is somehow anti-sex. Usually the narrative is about how European types like me were all naked and carefree and dancing around maypoles until the evil Christian missionaries invaded and forced us to convert to their backward, repressed religion and replaced our love for sex with an undying lust for violence.[1] That perception is quickly dashed against the rocks, however, for anyone who takes the time to learn about any of the world's few remaining pre-Christian societies—it turns out that everyone, everywhere, has weird hang-ups about sex.[2]

---

1. That would explain whatever's going on with Mel Gibson, I guess.
2. See, for instance, Lynn Saxon's *Sex at Dusk: Lifting the Shiny Wrapping from Sex at Dawn* for a discussion of how the popular idea of "sexually liberated" hunter-gatherers is, at best, complicated.

And let's be honest—why *wouldn't* they? Sex, after all, is the means of producing the next generation, so any society that *doesn't* take it seriously would naturally have died out a long time ago. Very few cultures are "liberated" sexually; it's just that the ones with different hang-ups seem that way to outsiders.

So where does the perception that Christianity is unusually sexually repressed come from? Probably from Christians themselves, because no one is going to get it from the Bible. The Bible is a veritable cornucopia of sex scenes, both wholesome (at least to the extent that a sex scene can be wholesome) and depraved (at least to the extent that a sex scene can be depraved), and it even includes a book that's arguably nothing *but* a sex scene. There's so much of it, in fact, that I debated for weeks about how to divide it up for this book. I've gone ahead and front-loaded the less shocking stuff, mainly because I'm writing this book for a Christian publisher and I'm hoping my editor won't bother to read past this chapter. With that in mind, I've devoted this chapter to plain-vanilla sex; you'll find wall-to-wall penises[3] in chapter 5; finally, chapters 6 and 8 are devoted to prostitution and incest, respectively, so feel free to skip ahead if that's your jam. (I sincerely hope that's not your jam.)

But I'm going to start at the beginning, with the mother of all biblical sex scenes:

Song of Songs: An Ode to Sex (Maybe. Who Knows.)

There's a book in the "wisdom" section of the Old Testament (basically, the place where they keep all the poetry) called either

---

3. Enjoy that mental image, I guess.

"Song of Songs" or "Song of Solomon," depending on whom you ask.[4] It's a brief eight chapters long, but to a reader coming off of Proverbs and Ecclesiastes (or Job, if you're reading a Jewish Tanakh), it's like a slap in the face of sexiness. Like Proverbs and Ecclesiastes, though, it's traditionally attributed to King Solomon, the son of King David and the last king over a united Israel. Like his dad, Solomon was a prolific poet, but, with a harem of 1,300, he may have been even more prolific at gettin' busy. Song of Songs, then, is his attempt to combine those two interests with a poem that describes a sexual encounter or three in what was no doubt graphic detail for the first millennium BC—sort of the prototypical R&B slow jam. Following the title, it gets right to the point:

> Let him kiss me with the kisses of his mouth!
> For your love is **better than wine**. (Song of Songs 1:2)

Wow, get a room, you two.

> The king has brought me **into his chambers**. (verse 4b)

Oh, okay, cool. Guess you're good to go, then.

Once they're alone, Solomon's pen starts to go a little crazy with the Harlequin-esque euphemisms:

> Behold, you are beautiful, my love,
> behold, you are beautiful!

---

4. The full title, from the first line of the text, is "The Song of Songs, Which is Solomon's," or something like that, but who in the world has time to type all that? I'm already exhausted from just typing it once. (It's also occasionally referred to as "Canticles.")

Your eyes are doves
> behind your veil.

Your hair is like a flock of goats
> leaping down the slopes of Gilead.

Your teeth are like a flock of shorn ewes
> that have come up from the washing,

all of which bear twins,
> and not one among them has lost its young. (4:1–2)

One of the common dismissals of the Bible among the Internet Skeptic™ set is that it's the work of "Bronze Age goatherders." I've never understood quite how that made the Bible baaaaaad,[5] but I won't deny that it makes for some awkward pillow talk. In fairness, though, when the woman is called upon to praise her lover's appearance, she doesn't do a whole lot better:

His hands are disks of gold set with emerald.
His chest is a block of ivory covered with sapphires.
(5:14 GW)

This, by the way, is one of those verses where English translators start *really* reaching with the euphemisms. I've helpfully provided you with what might be the most blissfully ambiguous rendering, the God's Word translation, a 1995 version with loose ties to the Lutheran Church—Missouri Synod. The GW dances around this verse as hard as it can, probably because no one, anywhere, wants to imagine Lutherans having sex. The first

---

5. Do you get it? Because goats say "baa"? It is a hilarious animal joke.

line is bad (his hands are *disks*? is he a Powerpuff Girl?), but the second is far worse—having a pale, blocky chest covered in blue protrusions is hardly something you'd put on your OkCupid profile.

So what's the beloved really talking about? First of all, the Hebrew word translated "chest" here, *meeh*, doesn't really have an English equivalent. Various translations render it "loins" (NABRE), "stomach" (ISV), "abdomen" (NASB), or "chest," but none of these really captures the essence of *meeh*, which can refer to almost any body part below the waist.

All this starts to make sense, though, when you consider what ivory is. It doesn't actually come in *blocks*; it's not something you cut out of a quarry, like marble. You hack it off of an elephant's face, probably while a sad Sarah McLachlan song plays in the background, because poaching is bad, you monster. When you remember which male lower body part is tusk-shaped and occasionally has blue protrusions, it becomes pretty clear we're talking about a penis here,[6] which makes sense, since, when you think about it, we're all pretty much *always* talking about penises. This becomes even more striking when you realize that all of Song of Songs, not just the man's dialogue, is traditionally credited to Solomon, heavily implying that the whole long poem was just an elaborate excuse to brag about his boner.

So there you have it. Song of Songs is just one long sex scene, complete with the BC equivalent of a "throbbing manhood" line. Right? Maybe, if you're a creepy neo-Reformed pastor.

---

6. Tremper Longman III, *Song of Songs* (Grand Rapids: Eerdmans, 2001), 173.

Interestingly, though, both the Jewish and the Christian interpretive traditions have, historically, steered pretty clear of overly literal understandings of the text. The rabbinic tradition has almost universally taken Song of Songs as an allegory where the man represents God and the woman represents Israel[7]—not really that much of a stretch, considering that other parts of the Old Testament make frequent use of that exact metaphor.[8] Song of Songs, in fact, is the traditional synagogue reading for Passover, the holiest week in the Jewish calendar.

Similarly, Christian understandings of the text (going all the way back to even the earliest Christian theologians, like Origen of Alexandria) have regarded the man as a stand-in for Christ and the woman as a symbol of the church. Again, a reasonable reading, seeing how often that same metaphor pops up in the New Testament.[9] Other Christian readings of Song of Songs have reached even further than this, understanding it as a moral fable,[10] or even a gloss on the Holy Spirit and the Virgin Mary;[11] still, no matter how many allegorical layers you add, there's no escaping that Song of Songs is, on the surface, just a poem about Solomon having lots and lots of sex, by way of his very impressive boner. At some point, all the theologizing just becomes a way of insisting you only read the Bible for the articles.

---

7. H. H. Rowley, "The Interpretation of the Song of Songs," *Journal of Theological Studies* 38, no. 152 (1937): 337–63.

8. See Hosea 1:2; Ezekiel 16:8.

9. See Mark 2:19; John 3:29; Revelation 21:2.

10. E. Ann Matter, *The Voice of My Beloved: The Song of Songs in Western Medieval Christianity* (Philadelphia: University of Pennsylvania Press, 1992), 54.

11. Matter, 155.

IN TODAY'S HOT-TAKE TWITTER CULTURE, I NEED TO KNOW HOW TO FEEL ABOUT ST. PAUL, *NOW*

In his first epistle to the Corinthians, we learn that the apostle Paul is *very* much in favor of hot marital sex—at least, compared with the extramarital alternative. Husbands and wives should have sex, he says,

> For **the wife does not have authority over her own body**, but the husband does. (1 Corinthians 7:4a)

. . . thus proving that the Bible is chauvinistic and backward in every possible way. Paul then adds,

> **Likewise the husband does not have authority over his own body**, but the wife does. (verse 4b)

. . . thus proving how ultra-woke and totes relevant the Bible is. Now go forth and tweet.

Lot, Sodom, a Couple of Angels, and Some Very Awkward Propositions

But let's talk about one of those articles. Specifically, one where a couple of angels almost get gang-raped. No, really.

We all know what Sodom and Gomorrah were, right? Even if you're fuzzy on the specifics, you're probably vaguely familiar with the story: There were a couple of ancient cities that were so evil—either with sexual sin or a lack of hospitality, depending on whom you ask[12]—that God destroyed them with literal fire and brimstone. In the book of Genesis, though, there's a long narrative leading up to their destruction, mainly to demonstrate what a bunch of tool bags the men of Sodom (and, one assumes, Gomorrah) were.

Abraham's nephew, Lot, lives in Sodom, so before he destroys it, God sends a couple of angels to warn Lot and fam to literally run for the hills. The angels look for lodging, can't find any, and resolve to spend the night in the town square (there's that lack of hospitality), but Good Guy Lot sees them and invites them into his home. He cooks them some food, bakes them some unleavened bread (very trendy back then), and makes them as comfortable as he can. They're still munching their matzos, though, when things get real:

> But before they lay down, the men of the city, the men of Sodom, both young and old, all the people to the last man, surrounded the house. And they called to Lot, "Where are the men who came to you tonight? **Bring them out to us, that we may know them.**" (Genesis 19:4–5)

Hey, that's nice. Some new guys are in town, and the neighbors have turned out so they can get to know them. Right?

Ha, of course not. You're three chapters into this book now, so you should have guessed that **"know them"** is a euphemism for sex, because everything is a euphemism for sex. Actually, **"know them"**

---

12. Even the Bible as a whole has different perspectives on this. In Ezekiel 16:49, Sodom is condemned for failing to help the poor, while in Jude v. 7, Sodom is condemned for sexual sin. But, to quote an internet meme that will probably be stale before this book hits the presses, why not both?

is a fairly literal translation of the Hebrew *yadha*, which means "get acquainted with," but it frequently has a subtext of "*if you know what we mean.*"[13] There *are* English versions that try to force the carnal intent to the surface here—like the charmingly awkward "have relations with them" in the NASB, or the try-hard NIV's "have sex with them"—but invariably, the word choice ends up sounding like something your dad might imagine gang rapists saying.

In any case, based on his response, Lot doesn't seem to doubt the less-than-honorable intentions of the guys outside:

> Lot went out to the men at the entrance, shut the door after him, and said, "I beg you, my brothers, **do not act so wickedly.**" (verses 6–7)

Then he offers a solution that seems even worse than the original plan:

> "Behold, **I have two daughters** who have not known any man. Let me bring them out to you, and **do to them as you please.** Only do nothing to these men, for they have come under the shelter of my roof." (verse 8)

I guess it tells you all you need to know about Sodom that Lot—the one guy there who God deems worth saving—is the sort of guy whose response to "Can we rape your guests?" is "I'd be a *pretty lousy host* if I let you do that. Here, rape my daughters instead." Not that it *really* matters, since the rape mob's not particularly into the proposed idea:

---

13. Pim Pronk, *Against Nature? Types of Moral Argumentation Regarding Homosexuality* (Grand Rapids: Eerdmans, 1993), 268.

But they said, "Stand back!" And they said, "**This fellow came to sojourn, and he has become the judge!** Now we will deal worse with you than with them." Then they pressed hard against the man Lot, and drew near to break the door down. (verse 9)

In other words, "Who is *this guy* to tell us who we can and can't rape?" And then they bring out the battering ram. Because, sure, that's reasonable.

Fortunately, the angels are, as it happens, angels:

But the men reached out their hands and brought Lot into the house with them and shut the door. **And they struck with blindness the men who were at the entrance of the house,** both small and great, so that they wore themselves out groping for the door. (verses 10–11)

Weird to think that blindness would make them forget where the door is, but I guess magic angel blindness is different from the regular Stevie Wonder kind. In any case, the angels use this time they just bought to warn everyone of Sodom's impending doom, and Lot and his family escape the next day, unraped. No thanks to Lot's efforts, but still.

ON BOOBS, YOUR ELDERLY WIFE'S

In the book of Proverbs, King Solomon warns men not to stray from their wives (which seems super easy to say if you have six hundred wives to choose from, but I digress):

> Let your fountain be blessed,
>> and **rejoice in the wife of your youth**,
>> a lovely deer, a graceful doe. (Proverbs 5:18–19a)

Aw, that's cute. Thanks, Solomon.

>> **Let her breasts fill you at all times with delight**;
>> be intoxicated always in her love. (verse 19b)

. . . and that's less cute. More like the times your parents tried to tell you about the night you were conceived. Ew.

Jael Nails a Guy

If there's any doubt that rape and God's vengeance go together like peanut butter and crippling depression, you need look no further than chapter four of Judges for yet another example. The narrative found there, which directly follows the story of Ehud (see chapter 1), is not only needlessly grisly but is also one of the few times the Bible gets close to passing the Bechdel Test.[14] So there's that.

---

14. In case you're unfamiliar, the Bechdel Test was (somewhat inadvertently) created by cartoonist Alison Bechdel in 1985 in her comic strip *Dykes to Watch Out For*. The test, originally applied to movies, is as follows: Does the movie have (1) at least two female characters, who (2) have at least one conversation with each other, (3) about something other than a man? It's a pretty simple test, but it's almost shocking how few movies pass it.

The main character of the story, at least initially, is a prophetess/judge named Deborah, whose main schtick is hanging out under a palm tree, arbitrating disputes between Israelites, and going thus-saith-the-Lord on people's butts when they get out of line. As frequently happens (in Judges and elsewhere), Israel is under the thumb of an oppressive foreign power—in this case, the Canaanites—and, as judge over Israel, it's kind of Deborah's job to do something about it. She's not exactly Xena,[15] though, so—sorry, Strong Female Character™ fans[16]—she recruits a man to do it:

> **She sent and summoned Barak the son of Abinoam** from Kedesh-naphtali and said to him, "Has not the LORD, the God of Israel, commanded you, '**Go, gather your men** at Mount Tabor, taking 10,000 from the people of Naphtali and the people of Zebulun. And I will draw out Sisera, the general of Jabin's army, to meet you by the river Kishon with his chariots and his troops, and **I will give him into your hand**'?" (Judges 4:6–7)

Barak's response is somewhere along the lines of "But Mommmmmm":

> Barak said to her, "If you will go with me, I will go, but if you will not go with me, I will not go." (verse 8)

Deborah and/or God gets pretty annoyed that Barak needs a woman to hold his hand, even after he's been promised victory, so Deborah prophesies further:

---

15. I really need to update my pop culture references.
16. Things do get more Strong-Female-Character™y later in the story, I promise.

And she said, "I will surely go with you. Nevertheless, the road on which you are going will not lead to your glory, for **the LORD will sell Sisera into the hand of a woman.**" (verse 9a)

And that's pretty much how things go. Barak handily dispatches the Canaanites, but Sisera, their general, escapes on foot. Fortunately for him, he runs into someone who wants to help him out:

And Jael came out to meet Sisera and said to him, "Turn aside, my lord; turn aside to me; do not be afraid." So he turned aside to her into the tent, and **she covered him with a rug.** (verse 18)

Jael is portrayed as a Kenite, a tribe that was trying to maintain neutrality in the Israelite-Canaanite conflict,[17] which makes her a bit of a wild card here. At first, it's not clear whose side she's on:

And he said to her, "Please give me a little water to drink, for I am thirsty." So **she opened a skin of milk and gave him a drink** and covered him. (verse 19)

He asks for water; she gives him milk (*that's* service); but then things turn . . . (puts on sunglasses) . . . *sour*:

But Jael the wife of Heber took a tent peg, and took a hammer in her hand. Then she went softly to him **and drove the peg**

17. J. David Schloen, "Caravans, Kenites, and Casus belli: Enmity and Alliance in the Song of Deborah," *Catholic Biblical Quarterly* 55, no. 1 (1993): 18–38.

into his temple until it went down into the ground while he was lying fast asleep from weariness. **So he died.** (verse 21)

The passage doesn't make it entirely clear why Jael felt the need to do this (apart from a desire to end the battle in the most awesome way possible[18]), but many commentators have observed that, in the larger context, it's strongly implied that a rape took place.[19] If you flip forward a chapter, you'll find a victory song sung by Deborah and Barak that describes the death of Sisera as follows:

> "Between her **feet**
>> he **sank**, he **fell**, he **lay** still;
> between her **feet**
>> he **sank**, he **fell**;
> where he **sank**,
>> there he **fell**—dead." (5:27)

Taken literally, this song seems to directly contradict what we read in the previous chapter. Sisera didn't "fall" at anyone's feet; he was already asleep, on the ground, before Jael killed him. However, you'll probably recall that words like **feet** and **lay** are common sexual euphemisms in Hebrew[20]—and the Babylonian Talmud makes this even more explicit, claiming Sisera raped Jael not once, but seven times (once for each euphemism).[21] Nor is the

---

18. A worthy goal in itself, to be sure.
19. Sarah Palmer, "Recovering Female Authors of the Bible," *Studia Antiquia* 15, no. 1 (2016): 13–26.
20. Susan Niditch, "Eroticism and Death in the Tale of Jael," in *Women in the Hebrew Bible: A Reader*, ed. Alice Bach (New York: Routledge, 1999), 305–16.
21. Babylonian Talmud *Yebamot* 103A.

idea that Sisera raped Jael at all far-fetched when you consider that rape was (and is!) considered, by many terrible people, to be the natural spoils of war. No doubt Sisera had been gearing up for some raping all morning and—having lost the battle—was trying to make the best ("best") of a bad situation.

Then she made the best of *that* situation by killing him in the face.

ON BLOODY SHEETS, THE USEFULNESS OF

The law of Moses offers fathers the following recourse when their sons-in-law accuse them of giving them nonvirgins for wives:

> And the father of the young woman shall say to the elders, "I gave my daughter to this man to marry, and he hates her; and behold, he has accused her of misconduct, saying, 'I did not find in your daughter evidence of virginity.' And yet this is the evidence of my daughter's virginity." **And they shall spread the cloak before the elders of the city**. (Deuteronomy 22:16-17)

They prove their daughters' virginity by *showing the bloody sheets to the village elders*. Aside from being mortifying for the bride, it seems like this would be really easy to fake, but Moses is the lawgiver, so I'll defer to him, I guess.

Sarai to Abram: "Here, Rape My Slave"

So by now you're probably starting to understand that the ancient world was basically a sexual free-for-all, where the rules applied only to those who couldn't afford to bend them (which I guess makes it exactly like the modern world). Not even Abraham, the first patriarch of Israel, was above this stuff.

In Genesis 16, Abram—who was to Abraham kind of what Jefferson Airplane was to Jefferson Starship[22]—finds himself in a bit of a pickle.[23] God has promised him countless descendants, but so far he doesn't have a single kid to his name—not even a bit of morning sickness for his wife, Sarai (who was to Sarah what Cassius Clay was to—never mind, you get it). But Sarai/h thinks she has the perfect solution:

> And Sarai said to Abram, "Behold now, the LORD has prevented me from bearing children. **Go in to my servant**; it may be that I shall obtain children by her." And Abram listened to the voice of Sarai. (Genesis 16:2)

As is frequently the case, this passage is somewhat euphemistic, but I'm kind of fascinated by how the euphemism just makes it sound that much more horrible. ("I'm not saying *rape* my slave; just *go into* her. I mean, *in to* her. You know what I mean.") Fortunately—and unusually for the book of Genesis—we're

---

22. A couple of chapters after this, God tells him to change his name from "Abram," which means "exalted father," to "Abraham," which means "father of many." (See? Totally different.)

23. Heh.

spared a graphic sex scene. And the plan seems to work, at least at first:

> And he went in to Hagar, and **she conceived**. And when she saw that she had conceived, **she looked with contempt on her mistress**. (verse 4)

Whoops, I can't imagine why Hagar would be bitter about this whole thing.[24] Sarai can't either:

> And Sarai said to Abram, "May the wrong done to me be on you! I gave my servant to your embrace, and when she saw that she had conceived, she looked on me with contempt. **May the LORD judge between you and me!**" (verse 5)

Wait, are you . . . are you *sure* you want that, Sarai? You force your slave and your husband to have sex against their will, and now you're upset that your slave is being *mean* to you? Is that—do you—are you really expecting God to be on *your* side here?[25] Fortunately, at this point, Abram puts his foot down, and—

> But Abram said to Sarai, "Behold, your servant is in your power; **do to her as you please**." (verse 6a)

Haha, just kidding. *Obviously*, Abram does exactly what he's been doing throughout the narrative, which is continue to let

---

24. Honestly, millennials are so entitled. *[Checks notes.]* I have just been informed that Hagar was not technically a millennial.

25. This always confused me about Tupac's oft-borrowed line "Only God can judge me." I'd say odds are good you don't actually want that.

Sarai treat her slave like garbage (who knows, maybe his entire thought process here is "If I play my cards right, I might get to have sex with someone under the age of ninety again").

> Then Sarai dealt harshly with her, **and she fled from her**. (verse 6b)

Hagar flees out into the wilderness, which is never a good idea if you live in the desert, so that should give you a ballpark figure of just how desperate she is here. Her story doesn't quite end there, though:

> **The angel of the LORD found her** by a spring of water in the wilderness, the spring on the way to Shur. And he said, "Hagar, servant of Sarai, where have you come from and where are you going?" (verses 7–8a)

Long story short, God promises to make Hagar into a great nation just like he promised Abram, and then he tells her to go back to Sarai, which probably sounds like awful advice, but given that her only other choice is to starve in the desert, I guess it makes sense. In any case, Hagar seems okay with it:

> So she called the name of the LORD who spoke to her, "You are a God of seeing," for she said, **"Truly here I have seen him who looks after me."** (verse 13)

Commentators, by the way, have been quick to point out that the first person in Scripture allowed to give God a name is an exiled slave girl.[26] God changes Abram's and Sarai's names; Hagar is allowed to change *God's* name. That tells you all you really need to know here about whose side God is on. In any case, Hagar returns to Abram and Sarai, gives birth to a son, and names him Ishmael, I assume because she's a big *Moby Dick* fan.

As a side note, if you're the sort of person who reads books or has a Hulu account, you might recognize this passage as the basis for Margaret Atwood's dystopian novel *The Handmaid's Tale*, which depicts a sinister American Christian theocracy in which "handmaids" are forced into sex slavery to help childless couples conceive. This is the sort of behavior you would expect from Christians who have read Genesis 16:2 and literally no other verse in the Bible,[27] which always seemed far-fetched to me, but recent political events have convinced me there are plenty of American Christians who haven't even read *that* much.

I HONESTLY WISH SOMEONE WOULD PUT THIS MUCH EFFORT INTO SEDUCING ME

In the book of Proverbs, author King Solomon is *very* concerned about thirsty girls:

And behold, the woman meets him,
dressed as a prostitute, wily of heart.
She is loud and wayward;

26. Thomas B. Dozeman, "The Wilderness and Salvation History in the Hagar Story," *Journal of Biblical Literature* 117, no. 1 (1998), 23–43.
27. In fairness, one sentence is about how much of *The Handmaid's Tale* I've read.

> her feet do not stay at home;
>
> now in the street, now in the market,
>
> and at every corner she lies in wait.
>
> **She seizes him and kisses him**,
>
> and with bold face she says to him,
>
> "I had to offer sacrifices,
>
> and today I have paid my vows;
>
> so now I have come out to meet you,
>
> to seek you eagerly, and I have found you.
>
> **I have spread my couch with coverings**,
>
> colored linens from Egyptian linen;
>
> **I have perfumed my bed** with myrrh,
>
> aloes, and cinnamon." (Proverbs 7:10–17)

I'm honestly not sure I believe that a woman has ever had to work this hard to score some casual sex, but there it is.

David and Bathsheba: It's Good to Be the King

But I'm bored with talking about what an embarrassment Abraham was. Let's talk about what an embarrassment David was! Again!

In case you've been skimming (jerk), here's a quick refresher: You know David. He killed Goliath. He watched Saul poop. He danced seminude. Somewhere in there, he became king of Israel. Oh, and he could also be a massive tool every now and then.

In the eleventh chapter of 2 Samuel, he's doing some draft dodging:

In the spring of the year, **the time when kings go out to battle**, David sent Joab, and his servants with him, and all Israel. And they ravaged the Ammonites and besieged Rabbah. **But David remained at Jerusalem.** (verse 1)

It's war season (which was apparently a thing in the ancient Near East[28]) and David the allegedly mighty man of war[29] is like, "Get to it, boys, I'm a conscientious objector." So while everyone else is out there accomplishing things and/or dying, David is at home being bored, which in the twenty-first century would mean lots of internet porn for him. That's not a thing yet, though, so David has to get involved in far more complicated shenanigans:

It happened, late one afternoon, when **David arose from his couch and was walking on the roof** of the king's house, that he **saw from the roof a woman bathing**; and the woman was very beautiful. (verse 2)

The woman, it turns out, is Bathsheba, which might be the most on-the-nose name anyone has ever given a Bible character.[30] Before we move on, though, we should probably take a second to underline *who* was on the roof in this narrative. In Western religious art (a genre whose practitioners will jump at any chance to paint someone naked), Bathsheba is frequently depicted as

---

28. Actually the explanation for this is pretty interesting, so I'll put it here: the reason was that harvest was in the spring, so there were fields full of grain for armies to loot and live on; going to war at any other time of year required an army to carry rations.
29. See 1 Samuel 16:18.
30. Yes, I know this joke only works in English. Sue me. (Please do not actually sue me.)

bathing on her own roof like some sort of exhibitionist,[31] but the passage makes it clear that *David* is the one on the roof. He's the creep; she's just trying to squeeze a quick shower in.

David starts asking around, finds out that she's the wife of one of his soldiers out on the front, and then proceeds to deal with the existence of an attractive woman the only way rich and powerful men know how:

> So David sent messengers and **took her**, and she came to him, and **he lay with her**. (verse 4a)

It's not explicitly stated in the text, but a lot of modern commentators will tell you that this encounter amounted to rape, even if physical violence wasn't directly involved.[32] If rape is sexual contact without consent, and David was the king with an armed guard at his disposal, there really wasn't any meaningful way for Bathsheba to say yes or no to the encounter. At the very least, it was a gross abuse of power. Oh, and it gets worse.

David gets his rocks off, tells Bathsheba he'll totally call her sometime, and then:

> And the woman conceived, and she sent and told David, **"I am pregnant."** (verse 5)

Haha, whoops.

The good news (if you want to call it that) is that, as king,

---

31. Jean-Léon Gérôme's 1889 oil-on-canvas *Bathsheba* is probably the worst offender here.
32. Alexander Izuchukwu Abasili, "Was It Rape? The David and Bathsheba Pericope Re-examined," *Vetus Testamentum* 61, no. 1 (2011): 1–15.

David has access to a whole slew of quick fixes for a problem like this. Obviously, the simplest solution is to make Uriah, Bathsheba's husband, think he's the baby-daddy, so David calls him back from the front:

> David sent word to Joab, "Send me Uriah the Hittite." . . . Then David said to Uriah, "Go down to your house and **wash your feet**." (verses 6a, 8)

"Wash your feet" might be the most uncomfortable euphemism for sex yet, but there it is. Good Guy Uriah leaves David's court grateful for the leave but decides not to go home after all:

> But Uriah **slept at the door of the king's house with all the servants** of his lord, and did not go down to his house. (verse 9)

This leads to a whole vaudeville routine where David tries repeatedly to ask Uriah why he won't just go down to his house and inseminate his wife already, without, uh, actually saying those words:

> When they told David, "Uriah did not go down to his house," David said to Uriah, "Have you not come from a journey? Why did you not go down to your house?" Uriah said to David, "The ark and Israel and Judah dwell in booths, and my lord Joab and the servants of my lord are camping in the open field. Shall I then go to my house, to eat and to drink and to **lie with my wife**? As you live, and as your soul lives, I will not do this thing." (verses 10–11)

So, points for picking up on the subtext; fewer points for picking up on the urgency. David's not ready to give up, though, and he thinks maybe a bit of binge-drinking will weaken this weirdo's patriotic resolve[33]:

And David invited him, and he ate in his presence and drank, so that **he made him drunk**. And in the evening he went out to lie on his couch with the servants of his lord, **but he did not go down to his house**. (verse 13)

As we all know, though, the problems you can't solve with sex and drinking can always be solved with cartoonishly cold-blooded murder:

In the morning David wrote a letter to Joab and sent it by the hand of Uriah. In the letter he wrote, **"Set Uriah in the forefront of the hardest fighting, and then draw back from him, that he may be struck down, and die."** (verses 14–15)

The Israelite army bumps off Uriah in what might be the most Wile E. Coyote–esque way possible, he comes home in a pine box, and David is like, "Cool, now I can propose to his pregnant widow." Which he does. Naturally, God is not super okay with all this, and he sends the prophet Nathan to tell David a parable about a rich guy who stole a poor guy's sheep, because sheep are literally the only metaphor that David understands for anything. (Read the Psalms if you think I'm joking.) Upon hearing the story, David says he's super-extra sorry, and

---

33. It's somewhat ironic that Uriah, as a Hittite, has more patriotism for Israel than the freaking king of Israel.

God tells him it's cool and the only one who will be dying in the immediate future is the baby. Which hardly seems fair, but there it is.

ON YOUR AMAZING TECHNICOLOR DREAMCOAT, FUN WAYS TO LOSE

In the thirty-ninth chapter of Genesis, noted garment aficionado Joseph finds himself pursued by his slave master's very thirsty wife:

> But one day, when he went into the house to do his work and none of the men of the house was there in the house, she caught him by his garment, saying, **"Lie with me."** (verses 11–12a)

I guess she should have put a bit more effort into that seduction attempt (maybe get some tips from that adulteress in Proverbs?), because Joseph responds by bolting out the front door. When they find her clutching his robe, she puts a comparable amount of effort into her alibi:

> "He came in to me to lie with me, and I cried out with a loud voice. And as soon as he heard that I lifted up my voice and cried out, **he left his garment beside me and fled** and got out of the house." (verses 14b–15)

> But of course it works, and Joseph gets thrown in prison,
> because in a case of he-said-she-said, you always side
> with whoever's rich and famous.

Rachel's Period Saves the Day[34]

Between Bathsheba and Hagar, the women have gotten kind of a raw deal in the last couple of stories, so let's finish strong with one where only a woman could have saved the day.

This story is about Rachel, whom I'll talk about a bit more in chapter 8. She was the wife of Jacob, who was the last major biblical patriarch (i.e., Isaac's son; i.e., Abraham's grandson). Or, rather, she was *one* of his wives, because he also married her sister, because, Old Testament. Oh, and also, she was his cousin, because—you get it.

Anyway.

There's a whole long narrative leading up to this moment, where Jacob has been crashing with his uncle Laban and marrying his various daughters, but fish and guests smell after three days, and Jacob's been there for decades, so Laban's starting to resent him a bit. Jacob says, "Hey wives/cousins, I think we should pack up and flee for our lives," and they escape in the middle of the night to avoid one of those crazy uncle tantrums. The plan probably would have gone off without a hitch, except:

---

34. Yes, I know menstruation and sex aren't the same thing; there's just no better place for this one.

Laban had gone to shear his sheep, and **Rachel stole her father's household gods**. (Genesis 31:19)

Laban wakes up, discovers that someone has literally stolen his gods (laugh if you want, but many ancient religions believed that the god's spirit was physically contained within the idol[35]), and chases after them with all the fury of a spurned uncle and all the additional fury of a spurned father-in-law. He's actually ready to kill them all on the spot, but then God (yeah, *that* God) tells him in a dream that his plan would be a bad idea. So when he catches them, he tries using his words instead:

"And now you have gone away because you longed greatly for your father's house, but **why did you steal my gods?**" (verse 30)

Jacob, as a patriarch, has personal conversations with the literal God of the universe on a surprisingly regular basis, so he's pretty confident he didn't steal any idols. He invites Laban to search the entire camp:

"**Anyone with whom you find your gods shall not live.** In the presence of our kinsmen point out what I have that is yours, and take it." Now Jacob did not know that Rachel had stolen them. (verse 32)

---

35. Julian Jaynes, *The Origin of Consciousness in the Breakdown of the Bicameral Mind* (Boston: Houghton Mifflin, 1976), 140.

Those of us in the storytelling business[36] call this "dramatic irony"—it's when a character makes a tragic decision based on his own ignorance of something the audience knows.[37] Laban starts searching the tents, one by one, and soon Rachel's is the only one left. Fortunately, she's thinking with her . . . butt:

> Now Rachel had taken the household gods and **put them in the camel's saddle and sat on them**. (verse 34a)

My research tells me that camels have humps, which means that camel saddles tend to be rounded, quasi-freestanding things with a lot of space inside them—apparently enough space to hide a whole stash of idols. Anyway, you get it. You went to the zoo as a kid.[38]

I'm not about to suggest that this was the *ideal* plan. Laban's been tearing the tents apart with abandon and not long ago was seriously contemplating mass murder. It's probably a tiny bit optimistic to imagine he won't have the stones to just ask Rachel to stand up. Fortunately, though, she's on top of that (in addition to being on top of a camel saddle stuffed full of idols):

> And she said to her father, "Let not my lord be angry that I cannot rise before you, for **the way of women is upon me**." (verse 35a)

---

36. I'm not saying you should buy my novel *Ophelia, Alive*, but you should definitely buy my novel *Ophelia, Alive*.
37. I know it's basically impossible to call something "irony" without setting off a Twitter storm of pedants determined to argue about it, but I'm banking on my suspicion that people who have time to argue about stupid stuff on Twitter don't read a lot of books.
38. How did zoos become synonymous with childhood? It must have been the marketing genius of some old-timey, nineteenth-century salesman. I assume the pitch involved a boater and the words "Step right up."

"The way of women" is a pretty literal translation of the Hebrew here, but in case you can't handle subtlety, the New International Version renders the line more straightforwardly as **"I'm having my period"**; the best version, though, comes from the International Standard Version, which has Rachel say, **"It's that time of the month,"** like some sort of '90s sitcom character.[39] In any case, Laban says, "Eew, never mind," and slinks out of the tent:

So he searched but **did not find the household gods**. (verse 35b)

Laban leaves empty-handed, but not before Jacob gives him a serious lecture about making ridiculous (i.e., technically true) accusations about the guy who watched his sheep for twenty years. And everything works out fine because Rachel managed to fake a period exceptionally well. Even in a heavily patriarchal society, women still sometimes come out on top.

And if you think that was a double entendre, *you're part of the problem.*

Jerk.

---

39. I mean, her name is Rachel, so . . .

CHAPTER FOUR

AND NOW FOR SOMETHING COMPLETELY VIOLENT

Horrific Violence, Some of It Involving Bears

In 2013, the journal *Pediatrics* published a study that found movies rated "PG-13" were, on average, *more* violent than movies rated "R."[1] The reason for this, as far as anyone can tell, is that it's easy to make violent acts *seem* less violent simply by neglecting to show their consequences. If your heroes mow down rows and rows of nameless bad guys who don't bleed, that's "PG-13" violence; if your character gets a hole blown in his chest and slowly bleeds to death, that's "R" violence. Level whole cities if you want, as long as we don't have to think about the people who are now dead, maimed, or homeless.

It's possible this is a uniquely American phenomenon. We're

---

1. Brad J. Bushman, Patrick E. Jamieson, Ilana Weitz, and Daniel Romer, "Gun Violence Trends in Movies," *Pediatrics* 132, no. 6 (2013): 1014–18.

generally huge fans of violence here in the States (we routinely gun each other down in the streets for fun), but sex is icky (we have sex in the streets significantly less often, which I understand is the reverse of how things are done in Europe). Culture aside, though, it makes sense that violence would creep into entertainment more easily than sex—it's easy to draw bright lines around things like nipples and genitalia (so say my adventures in MS Paint, anyway), but it's never quite as clear where the boundaries are with physical combat.

And, of course, how much a culture clutches its pearls at violence tends to depend entirely on how much that culture has to *deal* with violence. There's violence in art and literature because there's violence in the world; if the biggest problem in your life is *depicted* violence as opposed to *actual* violence, you're one of the lucky few.

The Bible, for the most part, was *not* written by the lucky few. Many of its books were composed during dark times when violence was simply a fact of life, and the authors weren't really interested in glossing over evil in order to appease a bourgeois audience. This chapter will look at some of the Bible's grisliest parts—which, if you're American, will seem like a nice reprieve from all that icky sex.

After this, we'll dive into the even ickier sex. But for now:

Merry Christmas! Let's Murder a Whole City's Worth of Babies

It's safe to say that pretty much everyone knows the Christmas story, right? Jesus is born, in a barn, to a virgin mother (like you do); angels sing; shepherds and wise men show up; gold, frankincense, and myrrh get passed around like candy; a little boy plays a drum for some reason; and the night wind talks to little lambs, because, sure, that makes sense. Right?

Actually, the nativity story you probably think you know is cobbled together from a variety of sources. That little drummer boy originates from a 1941 carol by Katherine Kennicott Davis; "Do You Hear What I Hear?" was written in 1962 as a protest against—of all things—nuclear war.[2] Even the less fanciful aspects, though—the wise men, the shepherds—come from disparate sources and are usually smashed together at random, depending on the whims of whoever's in charge of this year's Christmas pageant. The idyllic parade of angels, shepherds, and assorted farm animals comes from the second chapter of Luke's gospel, while the wise men and/or magi and/or three kings come from Matthew 2, which is a whole lot . . . darker.

It starts out innocently enough, though:

Now after Jesus was born in Bethlehem of Judea in the days of Herod the king, behold, **wise men from the east came to Jerusalem**, saying, "Where is he who has been born king of the Jews? For we saw his star when it rose and have come to worship him." (Matthew 2:1–2)

Matthew skips pretty much everything we get from Luke, including the birth itself. No shepherds, no angels, no

---

2. Spencer Kornhaber, "The Apocalyptic Fear in 'Do You Hear What I Hear,'" *Atlantic*, December 16, 2015, https://www.theatlantic.com/entertainment/archive/2015/12/the-apocalyptic-fear-within-do-you-hear-what-i-hear/420459/.

manger—just "He was born, and then some wise guys showed up." The **wise men**, by the way, were almost definitely not "three kings." There's no mention of there being three of them, and Matthew's word for them is "magi," which suggests they were priests, probably of the Zoroastrian faith.[3] I'm assuming you're not here for a lecture on Zoroastrianism, but briefly, it was one of the world's earliest known monotheistic religions and is generally regarded to have had a strong influence on Judaism during the Jews' Babylonian exile.

In any case, these guys show up because they saw a particularly bright star in the sky (because what could that mean other than the birth of a monarch you need to visit ASAP?), and they immediately start asking around about this whole "newborn king" situation. Specifically, they ask King Herod the Great about it, which I'm sure seems like a super idea to them, but it actually isn't, seeing as at least half the mustache-twirling villains in the New Testament are named Herod. This one ("the Great") is no exception:

> When Herod the king heard this, **he was troubled**, and all Jerusalem with him. (verse 3)

I used to wonder why Jerusalem itself would be **"troubled"** along with Herod, but when you're ruled by a despot, *his* problems tend to be yours, whether you want them to be or not. In other words, there's a deadly temper tantrum coming. Herod, after consulting his priests and scribes, directs the magi toward Bethlehem, and then adds this not-at-all-suspicious caveat:

---

3. Delmar Rodabaugh, "How the Magi Became Kings," *Western Humanities Review* 25, no. 3 (1971): 256.

And he sent them to Bethlehem, saying, "Go and search dili-
gently for the child, and **when you have found him, bring me
word, that I too may come and worship him.**" (verse 8)

The magi are apparently unfamiliar with the phenomenon of
evil politicians trying way too hard to sound pious, because they
tell Herod "Okay, sure," and head off. So now you know the terrible
truth about those adorable wise men from that crèche your mom
had: they didn't only bring a pile of gold and frankincense to baby
Jesus; they practically led a murderous dictator right to his door.

Of course, there's good news for baby Jesus in this story:

Now when they had departed, behold, an angel of the Lord
appeared to Joseph in a dream and said, "Rise, take the child
and his mother, and **flee to Egypt**, and remain there until I
tell you, for Herod is about to search for the child, to destroy
him." (verse 13)

So Jesus and fam escape to Egypt, and everything works out.
Oh, except for this:

Then Herod, when he saw that he had been tricked by the wise
men, became furious, and he sent and **killed all the male children in Bethlehem** and in all that region who were two years
old or under, according to the time that he had ascertained
from the wise men. (verse 16)

If you're horrified by this, you might be reassured to know that
many modern historians doubt Herod's so-called Massacre of the
Innocents actually happened. No ancient historian mentions it, and

some have argued that Matthew includes it here mainly to draw an analogy between Jesus and Moses (who, as a newborn, famously escaped Pharaoh's attempt to murder all male Israelite babies).[4] That doesn't mean Matthew was just making stuff up, though—as others have pointed out, first-century Bethlehem's males-under-two population would have comprised, at most, twenty kids.[5] Still an atrocity, to be sure, but compared to the numerous other atrocities Herod committed, it barely moves the needle[6]—not the sort of thing your average historian would have felt the need to mention, even if true.[7]

Also, for whatever it's worth: if you find it a bit strange that Christians callously shrug off the fact that Christ's birth resulted in the murder of a couple dozen kiddos, you might be reassured to know that Christianity has traditionally regarded said kiddos as the "first martyrs" of the faith, celebrating them annually on December 28,[8] the "Feast of the Holy Innocents (That Is, a Feast in Honor of the Holy Innocents, Not a Feast Where We Eat Holy Innocents, Because That Would Be Weird, How Weird Do You Think We Are—Okay, You Get It)." Historically, celebrations of Holy Innocents' Day have involved children and adults switching places,[9] along with smatterings of practical jokes à la April Fools'

4. Raymond Edward Brown, *An Adult Christ at Christmas: Essays on the Three Biblical Christmas Stories* (Collegeville, MN: Liturgical Press, 1988), 11.

5. Raymond Edward Brown, *The Birth of the Messiah: A Commentary on the Infancy Narratives in the Gospels of Matthew and Luke* (New York: Doubleday, 1999), 104–21.

6. Everett Ferguson, *Backgrounds of Early Christianity* (Grand Rapids: Eerdmans, 2003), 390.

7. R. T. France, *The Gospel of Matthew* (Grand Rapids: Eerdmans, 2007), 83.

8. Some traditions observe it on December 27 or January 10 instead.

9. Shulamith Shahar, "The Boy Bishop's Feast: A Case Study in Church Attitudes toward Children in the High and Late Middle Ages," *Studies in Church History* 31 (1994): 243–60.

Day.[10] Kind of a strange way to mark the anniversary of a mass murder, but no stranger than most holiday celebrations are, I guess.[11]

ON MEALS TO DIE FOR

One of the recurring themes in the latter books of Moses is how whiny the Israelites become after they've been rescued from slavery in Egypt. (Moses was, presumably, engaging in a bit of venting.) In Numbers 11, the people are sick of manna and demanding meat, so God sends them a flock of quail to hunt. But then:

> **While the meat was yet between their teeth**, before it was consumed, the anger of the LORD was kindled against the people, and **the LORD struck down the people with a very great plague**. (Numbers 11:33)

I think the lesson here is to never demand real meat, which is good advice whether you're in the Old Testament or at a Taco Bell.

---

10. José F. Blanco and Raúl J. Vázquez-López, "King Herod's Masked Soldiers Costumes at the Festival de Máscaras de Hatillo," *Journal of the Costume Society of America* 36, no. 1 (2010): 41–62.

11. Not to belabor the point, but can we talk about this for a sec? There are way too many people out there who point to things like Christmas trees (actually a sixteenth-century invention, but whatever) and say, "See??? *Proof* that Christmas is secretly a pagan holiday!!! What do *trees* have to do with *Jesus*???" But what holiday has ever had traditions that are obviously connected to what it celebrates? It's not like American troops defeated the British by grilling burgers, drinking cheap beer, and setting off Roman candles.

Elisha and the Murder-Bears

In the second chapter of 2 Kings, Elijah—regarded by many as the greatest prophet of the Old Testament—retires not just from prophecy but from life itself, in the most face-meltingly awesome way possible. Accompanied by his protégé, Elisha (tagline: "Elijah for people with speech impediments"), he treks into the wilderness, where he's taken up to heaven by a whirlwind and a chariot that's *literally on fire*, because [insert heavy metal guitar solo here]. Once he's gone, Elisha takes up his mantle. No, literally:

> **He took the mantle of Elijah that fell from him** and struck the waters and said, "Where is the Lord, the God of Elijah?" And when he also had struck the waters, they were divided here and there; and Elisha crossed over. (verse 14 NASB)

In case you're unaware, a **"mantle"** is an old-timey word for a sleeveless cloak. So now you know where that expression about "taking up a mantle" comes from, so, consider yourself educated. More important to the narrative here is the fact that, in dividing the waters, Elisha is performing the same miracle Elijah did a few verses ago, thus demonstrating his status as God's chosen successor. A few verses later, Elisha performs yet another miracle, purifying a polluted water source, and you'd think two miracles would be enough to prove his legitimacy as Israel's newest Big Prophet on Campus, but of course you'd be wrong. It's not long before the locals start jeering:

> He went up from there to Bethel, and while he was going up on the way, some **small boys** came out of the city and jeered

at him, saying, **"Go up, you baldhead! Go up, you baldhead!"** (verse 23)

Bald jokes? Clearly, these guys aren't messing around. Elisha responds the exact way any of us would: by cursing them. Things go south from there, though:

And he turned around, and when he saw them, **he cursed them** in the name of the LORD. And **two she-bears** came out of the woods and **tore forty-two of the boys**. (verse 24)

I can hear the pearl-clutchers already. "God murdered *children?* God is a *monster!*" And as I've said before, I'm not here to defend the Bible, but I do want to point out that there's a lot more going on in this passage than just "Isn't it *awesome* when kids get mauled by bears???"[12]

To start with, it's not entirely clear we're talking about kids per se here. The Hebrew phrase is *neurim qetannim*, which is probably better translated as "young men."[13] So we're talking about the high school track team, maybe, not some escapees from the local day care. Further, having a bald head, while it might seem like a goofy insult out of context, was considered a genuine mark of shame in ancient Israel,[14] sort of like wearing a

---

12. Let's be honest, though—there's nothing *un*awesome about bear maulings.

13. Nahum M. Sarna, "The Authority and Interpretation of Scripture in Jewish Tradition," in *Understanding Scripture: Explorations of Jewish and Christian Traditions of Interpretation*, ed. Clemens Thoma and Michael Wyschogrod (Mahwah: Paulist Press, 1987): 9–20.

14. David Penchansky, "Beauty, Power and Attraction: Aesthetics and the Hebrew Bible," in *Beauty and the Bible: Toward a Hermeneutics of Biblical Aesthetics,* ed. Richard J. Bautch and Jean-François Racine (Atlanta: Society of Biblical Literature, 2013): 47–66.

Creed shirt is today. And finally, Elisha's baldness as such was not the primary thing these guys were mocking. Elsewhere (2 Kings 1:8), his mentor Elijah is described as being hairy, so in mocking Elisha's baldness, they were actually questioning his legitimacy as Elijah's successor.[15]

There's an explicitly religious aspect to the mocking here as well. Elisha was on his way to Bethel, which was a major center of idol worship in Israel at the time,[16] possibly to continue Elijah's habit of berating King Ahab for engaging in said idol worship. In that sense, the taunting was less about the "baldhead" thing and more about the "go up" thing—i.e., "Haha, we'd like to see you *try* to prophet!" And then, he does. They're clearly not impressed by hippie stuff like water purification, so Elisha lets loose the most metal of his prophet powers.

Personally, though, I wonder if the whole bear-mauling thing was aimed at Elisha as much as anyone else. It's not like the guy was standing there practicing his bear calls; all he did was **"curse them"**—something a lot of us do without much thought on a daily basis. Then his words were immediately fulfilled in the most face-shredding way possible, reminding him that, as a prophet of the Lord, his words now carry a bit of heft. I'm sure people hesitated before mocking Elisha again, but I'm also sure *he* hesitated before cursing anyone again.

---

15. Fred E. Woods, "Elisha and the Children: The Question of Accepting Prophetic Succession," *Brigham Young University Studies* 32, no. 3 (1992): 47–58.

16. Joseph Blenkinsopp, "Bethel in the Neo-Babylonian Period," in *Judah and the Judeans in the Neo-Babylonian Period,* ed. Oded Lipschitz and Joseph Blenkinsopp (University Park, PA: Eisenbrauns, 2003), 93–108.

FRIENDS, ROMANS, COUNTRYMEN, ETC.

In Luke 22, when Jesus gets arrested, one of his disciples asks, "What would van Gogh do?"

> And one of them struck the servant of the high priest and **cut off his right ear**. (verse 50)

Before the disciple can finish the job, though, Jesus cuts in:

> But Jesus said, "No more of this!" **And he touched his ear and healed him.** (verse 51)

. . . which, I mean, is significantly more ballsy than cutting off the ear was.

No, God Will Totally Provide a Lamb: The Binding of Isaac

We've already spent quite a bit of time with Abraham in this book, which makes sense, since he's arguably the best candidate for the title "founder of Judaism." And yet, in the grand scheme of things, it's not like he did all that much. He didn't deliver the law, like Moses, or unite Israel for two generations of peace and prosperity, like David; he just helped conceive a single child and then raise him to adulthood. And, as we're about to see, he almost didn't even do *that*. Literally one chapter after Isaac is born, God comes to Abraham with . . . this:

> He said, "Take your son, your only son Isaac, whom you love, and go to the land of Moriah, and **offer him there as a burnt offering** on one of the mountains of which I shall tell you." (Genesis 22:2)

In a modern context, asking someone to murder his son to prove his love for you is probably a tad extreme, but keep in mind that the ancient Near East was more or less crawling with gods who demanded human sacrifice, often in the form of delicious children.[17] So really, it's not God who's being a weirdo in this story; if anything, it's just a case of him giving into peer pressure. Or at least—well, you'll see.

Abraham is surprisingly okay with the whole idea—you don't get to be a patriarch by spending a lot of time questioning the God of the universe—so he tells Isaac, "Hey, we're gonna go climb the mountain and sacrifice something to God, it'll be great," and Isaac is like, "Cool. Cookout with Dad. I love those." Then Abraham pulls one of the biggest jerk moves in the Old Testament:

> **And Abraham took the wood of the burnt offering and laid it on Isaac his son.** And he took in his hand the fire and the knife. So they went both of them together. (verse 6)

---

17. For a thorough discussion, see *Sacred Killing: The Archaeology of Sacrifice in the Ancient Near East*, ed. Anne Porter and Glenn M. Schwartz (University Park, PA: Eisenbrauns, 2012).

He makes Isaac carry the wood he's about to barbecue him on—and, just to be clear, he hasn't told him exactly what the plan is yet. Isaac's not entirely clueless, though:

> He said, "Behold, the fire and the wood, but **where is the lamb** for a burnt offering?" (verse 7b)

This would be the perfect time to come clean with his ~~victim~~ son, but Abraham keeps up the act, *and it works*:

> Abraham said, "**God will provide for himself the lamb** for a burnt offering, my son." So they went both of them together. (verse 8)

"God will provide for himself the lamb" is, in case you didn't know, one of the more iconic lines from the Bible, but in context, it's hard to know exactly what Abraham means by it. On its face, you could take it as simple, stoic resolve to trust God, even when the situation seems bleak; Christians have historically taken it as a prophecy, predicting the sacrifice of Christ (the *Lamb of God! get it???* you get it[18]); personally, I've always taken it to just be the laziest lie ever.

They get to the top of the mountain, and Abraham cuts to the chase:

> When they came to the place of which God had told him, Abraham built the altar there and laid the wood in order and **bound Isaac his son and laid him on the altar**, on top of the wood. (verse 9)

---

18. J. Edwin Wood, "Isaac Typology in the New Testament," *New Testament Studies* 14, no. 4 (1968), 583–89.

There's no mention of how Isaac reacts when dad starts tying him down to the altar, but I've always imagined him trying to bolt, and then Abraham chasing him around the altar repeatedly while "Yakety Sax" plays in the background. In any case, Abraham eventually gets the job done, and then things get super dark:

> Then Abraham reached out his hand and **took the knife to slaughter his son**. (verse 10)

But just as we're about to get an awesome description of blood and guts exploding everywhere, God puts a stop to the whole thing:

> But the angel of the LORD called to him from heaven and said . . . "**Do not lay your hand on the boy** or do anything to him, for now I know that you fear God, seeing you have not withheld your son, your only son, from me." (verses 11–12)

It was just a *test*! Get it? The good news is that PTSD apparently hasn't been invented yet, so Abraham and Isaac emerge from the experience basically okay, with the newfound knowledge that God is not the sort to demand child sacrifice (or at least not the sort to do so and *mean* it). And then the prophecy Abraham made earlier (you remember that one, right?) is fulfilled:

> And Abraham lifted up his eyes and looked, and behold, behind him was **a ram, caught in a thicket by his horns**. And Abraham went and took the ram and offered it up as a burnt offering instead of his son. (verse 13)

Abraham sacrifices the ram, and God tells Abraham that, now that he knows he'll obey him faithfully, he can *really* get started on that whole making-him-a-great-nation thing. And everything's cool, because Old Testament people ate god-induced trauma for lunch.

ON WHIPPING IT GOOD

In the gospel of John, Jesus unleashes all the fury of a half-sober Indiana Jones on everyone:

> In the temple he found those who were selling oxen and sheep and pigeons, and the money-changers sitting there. And **making a whip of cords, he drove them all out of the temple**, with the sheep and oxen. And he poured out the coins of the money-changers and overturned their tables. And he told those who sold the pigeons, "Take these things away; **do not make my Father's house a house of trade**." (John 2:14–16)

In case you missed it: *he made his own whip*. So not only is Jesus awesome—he's also crafty.

Eaten by Worms and/or Dogs

You're not tired of kings named Herod yet, are you? Good, because I have at least one more Herod story up my sleeve. This is a different Herod from either of the ones we've discussed previously, but one Herod is as good as another, right? They were all horrible; they all deserved to die horrible deaths. And some of them did! Enjoy.

This bit happens in the twelfth chapter of the Acts of the Apostles, which, if you're unfamiliar, is basically what the name implies: all the things the apostles did after Jesus ascended to heaven.[19] With Jesus gone, first-stringers like Peter and Paul go out into the world to make his message known—and some people, like King Herod Agrippa I,[20] bristle at their crazy new ideas, only to become worm food. No, literally.

After jailing some apostles, Herod goes off to give a speech at Caesarea. It goes pretty well:

> And the people were shouting, **"The voice of a god, and not of a man!"** (verse 22)

Herod doesn't bother to argue with them about this, which won't surprise you if you know anything about politicians, and God's response is a swift and merciless "Really, dude?":

> Immediately an angel of the Lord struck him down, because he did not give God the glory, **and he was eaten by worms and breathed his last**. (verse 23)

---

19. Pet peeve: A lot of people seem to confuse Jesus' resurrection and his ascension. For the record, the gospels record Jesus rising from the dead on Easter Sunday, appearing to his followers for a forty-day period (often sharing meals with them, letting them touch the wounds on his body, etc.), and then ascending to heaven, almost six weeks after the resurrection. My editor says this footnote is boring and needs a joke, so here you go: farts.

20. Dude needed to get A-grip-a. Right??? See, editor, this is the hacky stuff you get when you demand more jokes. I hope you're happy.

Maybe you're confused by the chronology here—he was eaten by worms and *then* died? That does appear to be the intended meaning, yeah. In *Antiquities of the Jews*, ancient historian Josephus seems to suggest Herod Agrippa was done in quickly and violently by some sort of intestinal parasite:

> **A severe pain also arose in his belly**, and began in a most violent manner. He therefore looked upon his friends, and said, "**I, whom you call a god, am commanded presently to depart this life** . . . When he said this, his pain was become violent. . . . When he had been quite worn out by the pain in his belly for five days, he departed this life. (Antiquities 19.346–350)

Meanwhile, Agrippa's predecessor, Herod the Great (the one who killed all the babies), appears to have died similarly:

> But now Herod's distemper greatly increased upon him after a severe manner, and this by God's judgment upon him for his sins; for a fire glowed in him slowly . . . for it brought upon him a vehement appetite to eating, which he could not avoid to supply with one sort of food or other. **His entrails were also ex-ulcerated**, and the chief violence of his pain lay on his colon; an aqueous and transparent liquor also had settled itself about his feet, and a like matter afflicted him at the bottom of his belly. Nay, further, **his privy-member was putrefied, and produced worms**. (Antiquities 17.168–169)

So, at least one Herod—possibly more—was *eaten to death by crotch worms.*

Old Testament villains, on the other hand, were more likely to be eaten by dogs, as happened to Elijah and Elisha's longtime rival, Queen Jezebel. In the ninth chapter of 2 Kings, revolutionaries led by a man named Jehu fight their way into her castle courtyard:

> And [Jehu] lifted up his face to the window and said, "**Who is on my side?** Who?" Two or three eunuchs looked out at him. He said, "Throw her down." **So they threw her down.** (verses 32–33a)

The horses get in on the fun too:

> And **some of her blood spattered on the wall and on the horses**, and **they trampled on her**. (verse 33b)

Then the revolutionaries break for lunch, or whatever, and when they come back:

> But when they went to bury her, **they found no more of her than the skull and the feet and the palms of her hands**. When they came back and told him, he said, "This is the word of the Lord, which he spoke by his servant Elijah the Tishbite: 'In the territory of Jezreel **the dogs shall eat the flesh of Jezebel**, and **the corpse of Jezebel shall be as dung** on the face of the field in the territory of Jezreel, so that no one can say, This is Jezebel.'" (verses 35–37)

So, there you have it. If you're an oppressive, blasphemous monarch, your crotch gets eaten by worms, or most of you gets eaten by dogs, or whatever. Which is good, because it's important to find a use for everything, and that trendy grain-free dog food isn't cheap.

ON THE JOYS OF BABY MURDER

Psalm 137 is a brief screed against the Babylonian Empire, who had recently invaded and destroyed Jerusalem. The last two verses do *not* waste time on subtlety:

> Daughter Babylon, doomed to destruction,
>> happy is the one who repays you
>> according to what you have done to us.
>
> **Happy is the one who seizes your infants**
>> **and dashes them against the rocks.** (verses 8–9 NIV)

This is one of the passages that gets held up as proof that *See, the Bible is horrible!!!* but it's a little more complicated than that, for a couple of reasons:

1. This is literally something Babylon had just finished doing to Israel.
2. Strictly speaking, nothing here *advocates* baby murder—all it says is that the guy who gets to do it will be *happy*. Is there any doubt that a guy who wanted to murder Babylonian babies would be happy when he finally got a chance to do it? I'm just saying.

Nadab and Abihu: Burn That Funky Incense Right

The book of Leviticus is mainly a list of instructions for how Israel was supposed to properly prepare and present their offerings to God, and it's every bit as scintillating as it sounds, so it's probably good that God throws in some pyrotechnics here and there:

> And **fire came out from before the LORD and consumed the burnt offering** and the pieces of fat on the altar, and when all the people saw it, they shouted and fell on their faces. (Leviticus 9:24)

God spends the book setting up an Israelite priesthood that will last for a few thousand years, so it makes sense that he would be going out of his way to show which offerings are acceptable *in the most awesome way possible*. If you get your offering right, God will light it up. And if you get it wrong, God will light *you* up:

> Now Nadab and Abihu, the sons of Aaron, took their respective firepans, and after putting fire in them, placed incense on it and offered **strange fire** before the LORD, which He had not commanded them. And **fire came out from the presence of the LORD and consumed them**, and they died before the LORD. (10:1–2 NASB)

Whoops.

"Strange," by the way, is a pretty literal translation of the Hebrew word *zarah* here. Most English translations render it **"unauthorized fire,"** which gets at the spirit of things, but I prefer to think of Nadab and Abihu as a couple of drunk rednecks, poking at their fire with sticks and saying, "That sure is some strange fire, I tell you what!" And actually, given the larger context of the passage, that interpretation probably isn't too far off:

> And the LORD spoke to Aaron, saying, "**Drink no wine or strong drink**, you or your sons with you, when you go into the tent of meeting, **lest you die**. It shall be a statute forever throughout your generations." (verses 8–9)

In other words, we appear to be dealing with a "Hold my beer and watch this!" scenario—God was lighting up offerings; people were falling on their faces; Nadab and Abihu were a little tipsy and wanted to get in on the pizzazz (and, presumably, the glory). Earlier, though, God was pretty clear that only Aaron the high priest had been authorized to present an offering:

> **Moses then said to Aaron**, "Come near to the altar and offer your sin offering and your burnt offering, that you may make atonement for yourself and for the people; then make the offering for the people, that you may make atonement for them, **just as the LORD has commanded**." (9:7 NASB)

All that is to say, that as sons of the high priest, these guys should have known better than to show up for work drunk and try to claim credit for the fire that was *literally falling from heaven*. That's probably why, a couple of verses later, Moses tells Aaron that he is *not allowed to mourn his dead sons*:

> And Moses said to Aaron and to Eleazar and Ithamar his sons, "Do not let the hair of your heads hang loose, and **do not**

tear your clothes, lest you die, and wrath come upon all the congregation; but let your brothers, the whole house of Israel, bewail the burning that the LORD has kindled." (10:6)

Moses was hard-core.

AND SPEAKING OF WHO SHOULD OR SHOULDN'T BE DRUNK

In the thirty-first chapter of the book of Proverbs, the (otherwise unknown) King Lemuel shares some thoughts from his mother on drinking:

> **It is not for kings, O Lemuel,**
>> **it is not for kings to drink wine,**
>>> or for rulers to take strong drink,
>>> lest they drink and forget what has been decreed
>>>> and pervert the rights of all the afflicted. (verses 4–5)

Which seems reasonable, but then Lemuel's mom adds this:

> **Give strong drink to the one who is perishing,**
>> **and wine to those in bitter distress;**
>>> let them drink and forget their poverty
>>>> and remember their misery no more. (verses 6–7)

So don't get drunk. Get poor people drunk!

Jephthah's Daughter: Worst Sweet Sixteen Ever

Of course, no chapter on violence would be complete without a visit to the book of Judges, which is basically nothing but violence from start to finish. As a reminder to anyone who's been skimming, Judges is a book about the same thing happening over and over again: Israel practices idolatry; God allows them to be conquered as punishment; God sends a "judge" to rebel against their conquerors.

Jephthah, who shows up in the eleventh chapter of the book, is the judge God calls upon to free Israel from the tyranny of the Ammonites. Before he rides into battle, though, he makes this not-at-all-reckless promise to God:

> And Jephthah made a vow to the LORD and said, "If you will give the Ammonites into my hand, then **whatever comes out from the doors of my house** to meet me when I return in peace from the Ammonites shall be the LORD's, **and I will offer it up for a burnt offering.**" (verses 30–31)

In case you weren't paying attention, Jephthah just took a vow that, if he wins the battle, he'll murder whatever walks out of his house first when he gets home. For God. Granted, this was an era when most people owned some sort of livestock, and many of them kept those animals in their houses,[21] but Jephthah *must* have realized there were about a thousand ways for this vow to go sideways, right? No?

---

21. Oded Borowski, *Every Living Thing: Daily Use of Animals in Ancient Israel* (Lanham, MD: Altamira Press, 1999), 45.

In any case, he *does* manage to defeat the Ammonites, and then his vow *does* go sideways, in probably the exact way you were expecting:

Then Jephthah came to his home at Mizpah. And behold, **his daughter came out to meet him** with tambourines and with dances. (verse 34a)

Not only does his daughter come out to greet him, she comes out *celebrating his victory*, because yay for tragic irony. Good thing kids are a dime a dozen—

She was his only child; besides her he had neither son nor daughter. (verse 34b)

—oops.

But unlike with the Abraham and Isaac story, God never steps in to prevent the human sacrifice from occurring. Interestingly, though, the passage never clearly says that Jephthah goes through with it—the text actually gets weirdly euphemistic here:

And she said to him, "My father, you have opened your mouth to the LORD; **do to me according to what has gone out of your mouth,** now that the LORD has avenged you on your enemies, on the Ammonites." So she said to her father, "Let this thing be done for me: leave me alone two months, that I may go up and down on the mountains and **weep for my virginity,** I and my companions." (verses 36–37)

You'll probably agree that this is a *weird* time for the passage to start dancing around reality. She's apparently not mourning her impending death—just that she's never gotten a chance to have sex. It's because of this surprising choice of words that a handful of commentators have suggested that Jephthah didn't actually *sacrifice* his daughter, but instead committed her to a lifetime of sexual abstinence and religious service.[22] That may sound like a bit of wishful thinking from people looking to sanitize Scripture, but they *do* have at least one halfway decent point on their side: back in verse 31, when Jephthah says, "**Whatever comes out from the doors of my house** . . . shall be the LORD's, **and I will offer it up for a burnt offering**," the Hebrew conjunction there doesn't necessarily mean "**and.**" It's often translated "**or,**"[23] rendering the phrase "shall be the LORD's, **or** I will offer it up for a burnt offering."

Of course, the problem with *that* interpretation is that it makes no sense—*either* he'll offer it as a burnt offering, *or* it will be the Lord's? Wouldn't it be the Lord's either way?

Regardless, the passage never mentions whether Jephthah goes through with the whole human sacrifice thing, but it does leave us with this:

> She had never known a man, and it became a custom in Israel **that the daughters of Israel went year by year to lament the daughter of Jephthah the Gileadite four days in the year.** (verses 39b–40)

---

22. David Marcus, *Jephthah and His Vow* (Lubbock, TX: Texas Tech University Press, 1986), 30.

23. Richard C. Steiner, "Does the Biblical Hebrew Conjunction -ו Have Many Meanings, One Meaning, or No Meaning at All?," *Journal of Biblical Literature* 119, no. 2 (2000): 249–67.

They give her an annual four-day festival, which seems a little excessive if the worst thing that ever happened to her was failure to get laid.

Then again, as you'll see when you turn the page, penises were a pretty big deal back then.[24]

---

24. I promise there are very few actual penises on the next page.

CHAPTER FIVE

TAKE A TIP FROM ME

Circumcision and More Phallic Phun!

Statistically, about half of you are reading this page with smoke pouring out of your ears. You saw the title of this chapter in the table of contents and tore past half the book's pages, blinded with rage, cursing my name and growling, "He thinks circumcision is *phun???* What even *is* 'phun'??? If it's anything like 'fun,' *I am so mad right now.*"

And look, I get it. It's not without reason that mentioning circumcision leaves people seething with fury even faster than mentioning veganism does. You believe in bodily autonomy. You don't think anyone's genitals should be modified without their explicit consent. Keep in mind, though, that the Bible simply doesn't have the same understanding of individual rights that modern thinking does—in the Bible, you're a part of a whole, not an autonomous orphan. God gave Abraham the practice of circumcision as a sign not just for him but for all of his descendants, generation after generation. In a very real sense, if you were part of Abraham's genetic line, you were already circumcised before you were born.

This actually stands in sharp contrast to most other cultures that have historically practiced circumcision. While many non-Jewish civilizations, mainly in the Middle East and Africa, have engaged in weenie-whacking, it's most often been done as a rite of passage for boys reaching ceremonial manhood.[1] The Jewish tradition subverts this by applying the practice to infants eight days old—with Jewish circumcision, you're marked as belonging to God not because of anything you've accomplished, but simply because God has chosen you. Biblical circumcision, then, is a reminder that, like it or not, you are part of something bigger than yourself. And possibly even bigger than your penis.[2]

Medical literature on the benefits and drawbacks of circumcision remains pretty thin,[3] but even if the practice confers no medical benefit, most studies have found it to be a fairly harmless operation with few risks associated.[4] So, that's reassuring, right? Can we all find something else to be unreasonably upset about? At the very least, can we try to relax a *little*?

I mean, you're deliberately reading a book about boner jokes in the Bible, so maybe stop taking yourself so seriously.

---

1. D. Doyle, "Ritual Male Circumcision: A Brief History," *Journal of the Royal College of Physicians in Edinburgh* 35 (2005): 279–85.
2. Not mine, though, obviously.
3. At the very least, it appears to have the modest effect of slowing the spread of some STDs—e.g., see John N. Krieger, "Male Circumcision and HIV Infection Risk," *World Journal of Urology* 30, no. 1 (2012): 3–13.
4. Helen A. Weiss, Natasha Larke, Daniel Halperin, and Inon Schenker, "Complications of Circumcision in Male Neonates, Infants and Children: A Systematic Review," *BMC Urology* 10, no. 2 (2010), https://bmcurol.biomed-central.com/articles/10.1186/1471-2490-10-2.

Circumcision 101, and the Importance of Having Uncrushed Balls

It takes the Bible only seventeen chapters to get around to circumcision, but a *lot* happens in those seventeen chapters. God creates the entire universe, humanity ruins it with sin, Cain invents murder (thanks a *lot*, Cain), God destroys the world, God re-creates the world, God invents different languages as a means of undermining ambitious construction projects, and Abraham's wife forces him to impregnate her slave. (It's a whole thing—see chapter 3.) So it takes God a while to get around to slicing up Abraham's ding-dong, but when he *does* get around to it, he's pretty serious:

> "Every male throughout your generations, **whether born in your house or bought with your money** from any foreigner who is not of your offspring, both he who is born in your house and he who is bought with your money, shall surely be circumcised. So shall my covenant be **in your flesh** an everlasting covenant. Any uncircumcised male who is not circumcised in the flesh of his foreskin shall be cut off from his people; he has broken my covenant." (Genesis 17:12b–14)

So, not just Abraham but *everyone*. If this all seems a tad weird and creepy and obsessive, that's because it is, but also keep in mind that the covenant God is making with Abraham is a *genetic* covenant. God's agreement with Abraham was that he would give him children, and grandchildren, and great-grandchildren, and so on, until his descendants were a great nation. In other words, this deal was inherently, inescapably penis-related. That the nation of Israel took this makin'-babies stuff seriously was very important to God, which might be why, when you get to the law of Moses a few books later, you get stuff like this:

> "No one whose **testicles are crushed** or **whose male organ is cut off** shall enter the assembly of the LORD." (Deuteronomy 23:1)

In context, this is the first item in a *long* list of restrictions of who can or can't enter the temple, but of course it's about genitals and of course it's weirdly specific. (A crushed penis or amputated testicles would presumably be fine, but *don't you dare* try to enter the temple with the reverse.) And maybe it's partly because of this restriction that we get stuff like this, just a couple of chapters later:

> "When men fight with one another and the wife of the one draws near to rescue her husband from the hand of him who is beating him and puts out her hand and **seizes him by the private parts**, then you shall **cut off her hand**. Your eye shall have no pity." (Deuteronomy 25:11–12)

Which—wait—was this a *thing* in ancient Israel? Were there just marauding bands of women helping their husbands win arguments by grabbing the other dude's junk? Was Israel just a never-ending episode of *America's Funniest Home Videos*? (I mean, I sure hope it was.) If the punishment seems harsh, though, consider the potential consequences of rampant ball-grabbing: if serious injury resulted from the act, not only would the poor guy be banned from the temple, but he wouldn't be able to contribute to Abraham's genetic line, which, again, was kind of a big thing.

I guess the punishment is pretty harsh, but still.

AHAB'S PALACE MUST HAVE SMELLED AWFUL

In 2 Kings 9, God tells the prophet Elisha to proclaim his everlasting curse on King Ahab's household:

> For the whole house of Ahab shall perish: and I will cut off from Ahab **him that pisseth against the wall**, and him that is shut up and left in Israel. (verse 8 KJV)

Most modern translations render this limply as **"every male,"** but the King James Version translates the Hebrew literally, because the King James Version is awesome. I can't help but wonder, though, why everyone was pissing against Ahab's walls, like his palace was freaking Versailles. Guy was a king, and he couldn't afford a single urinal?

Moses Drops the Ball

If you have any doubts that God takes circumcision *super* seriously, particularly in the Torah, all you have to do is flip over to Exodus and see what happens when Moses forgets to circumcise his kid. Keep in mind that Exodus is traditionally attributed to Moses himself—I'm just reminding you now so that you realize Moses was apparently as confused by all this as you're likely to be.

This all happens after Moses' famous encounter with the burning bush—you remember the burning bush, right? Even if you've never picked up a Bible, you've seen it in a movie. Moses, having escaped from Egypt, where the Israelites are enslaved, encounters God in the form of a bush that's on fire but won't burn up (it's a thing); God says, "Hey, I've chosen you to deliver my people from slavery"; Moses says, "Uh, nope"; God says, "Uh, yup"; finally, Moses gives in and heads back toward Egypt, accompanied by his wife Zipporah and his kiddos.

You know what comes next—the ten plagues, right? Well, sort of. Before we can get to *those*, God has to try to kill Moses.

No, really:

> At a lodging place on the way the Lord met him and **sought to put him to death**. (Exodus 4:24)

There's no transition here, by the way. The text goes straight from "God hired Moses to set his people free" to "God randomly tried to murder Moses at the Motel 6." The good news is that Zipporah—*somehow*—knows exactly what to do:

> Then Zipporah took a flint and **cut off her son's foreskin** and **touched Moses' feet with it** and said, "Surely you are a bridegroom of blood to me!" So he let him alone. (verses 25–26a)

Zipporah, as it happens, is the only non-Israelite in the room,[5] so it's interesting that she, of all people, is the one who figures out what the problem is. Her quick thinking seems to do the trick, though, because that's basically where the scene ends—in

---

5. If you're wondering, she's a Kenite, like Jael in chapter 3.

the next verse, Moses and fam are headed back to Egypt to take on Pharaoh again, as if nothing happened.[6]

If you think you're confused now, though, know that we're just getting started.

In the first place, exactly what transpired in this scene isn't even clear from the text. For instance, here's the King James version of the passage, where it's impossible to tell who's doing what:

> And it came to pass by the way in the inn, that the LORD met **him**, and sought to kill **him**. Then Zipporah took a sharp stone, and cut off the foreskin of her son, and **cast** it at **his** feet, and said, Surely a bloody husband art thou to me. So **he** let **him** go. (verses 24–26a KJV)

You'll notice that this version is just a parade of male pronouns, which is basically how the original Hebrew reads as well (modern translations that use names like "Moses" are making an editorial decision), so there's no way to know for sure what happens in the scene being described. The first couple of instances of **"him"** almost definitely refer to Moses—but whose feet is Zipporah throwing the foreskin at? And *why?*

Most recent translations assume she's throwing it at Moses' feet in anger or disgust, which is a reasonable guess. But she could just as easily be throwing it at her son's feet, or even *God's*

---

6. It's stuff like this that has led many scholars to conclude that the Torah was actually cobbled together from several disparate sources (this is referred to as the "Documentary Hypothesis," in case you want to look it up). Because, as anyone who's never read a Dan Brown novel knows, it's impossible for a single author to compose a work that's disjointed and amateurish.

feet, since God, especially in the Torah, is occasionally depicted as appearing with a body.[7] Complicating things further is the fact that the word translated **"cast"** here, *wattagga*, can also be rendered "touched" ("Zipporah touched it to his feet"),[8] or even "fell" ("Zipporah fell at his feet").[9] So it's possible that, rather than throwing the foreskin at Moses in a fit of rage, she's falling at God's feet and begging for mercy, or maybe performing an obscure (and otherwise unknown) ritual where the foreskin was touched to the child's feet. Or his father's. Or . . . God's?

But you've read the previous chapters, so you know that "feet" is often used, in ancient Hebrew, as a euphemism for "genitals." That opens up some even more uncomfortable interpretations of this passage, like maybe Zipporah is touching her son's foreskin to her husband's genitals (perhaps to emphasize the inherited covenant?)—or even God's. Does God have genitals? I have no idea. Maybe!

Regardless of exactly how the circumcision went down, though, there's still a gaping question these three verses leave unanswered: How in the world did Zipporah figure out what the problem was? God showed up, started murdering her husband without explanation, and she just managed to make a lucky guess?

I don't have a definitive answer for you on this one, but the ancient Hebrew text Exodus Rabbah posits one, which I swear I am not making up: apparently, God appeared as a giant serpent and attempted to kill Moses in a *very* specific way—by swallowing him headfirst, up to his genitals, spitting him out, and then swallowing

---

7. Michael S. Heiser, *The Unseen Realm: Recovering the Supernatural Worldview of the Bible* (Bellingham, WA: Lexham Press, 2015), 134.

8. Hans Kosmala, "The 'Bloody Husband,'" *Vetus Testamentum* 12, no. 1 (1962): 14–28.

9. John T. Willis, *Yahweh and Moses in Conflict: The Role of Exodus 4:24–26 in the Book of Exodus* (Bern, Switzerland: Peter Lang AG, 2010), 154.

him once more, genital-high again, this time from the feet up.[10] This was evidently enough of a hint for Zipporah, who concluded it was time for a circumcision, and not just time to lay off the absinthe.

GOD'S CROTCH IS DANGEROUS

In the eighth chapter of the prophecy of Ezekiel, the eponymous prophet comes face-to-face with God (so to speak):

> Then I looked, and behold, a form that had the appearance of a man. **Below what appeared to be his waist was fire**, and above his waist was something like the appearance of brightness, like gleaming metal. (verse 2)

So apparently, God's junk is perpetually on fire. Which is cool.

Rehoboam and the Posthumous Schlong-Measuring Contest

I want to take a break from circumcision for a sec, but let's stay on the subject of father-son penis interactions, since that seems like fertile[11] ground for discussion. Before we do that, though, we

---

10. Babylonian Talmud Nedarim 32a; Exodus Rabbah 5:5.
11. Heh.

need to discuss ancient Israelite politics for a moment, so try to contain your excitement (if you can).

Following the period of the judges, Israel is united as a kingdom under a grand total of three kings—Saul, David, and Solomon—and then things go south fast. After Solomon's death, his son Rehoboam is set to ascend to his throne, but on the eve of his coronation, a delegation is sent to tell him:

> **"Your father made our yoke heavy.** Now therefore lighten the hard service of your father and his heavy yoke on us, and we will serve you." (1 Kings 12:4)

"Hey, your dad treated us like slaves," they say. "Can you, maybe, *not* do that so much?" Rehoboam strokes his chin thoughtfully and consults his dad's old policy advisors, who tell him:

> "If you will be a servant to this people today and serve them, and speak good words to them when you answer them, then they will be your servants forever." (verse 7)

It's a basic principle of leadership, after all: if you prove you're a servant to your followers, they'll accompany you to hell and back. Rehoboam decides he'd like a second opinion, though, so he consults the wisest men he knows, by which I mean his drinking buddies, who tell him:

> "Thus shall you speak to this people who said to you, 'Your father made our yoke heavy, but you lighten it for us,' thus shall you say to them, '**My little finger is thicker than my father's thighs.** And now, whereas my father laid on you a

heavy yoke, I will add to your yoke. My father disciplined you with whips, but I will discipline you with scorpions.'" (verses 10b–11)

Which seems like a great plan that could not possibly backfire in any possible way.

You can probably guess where this is going. Rehoboam's 2:00 a.m. tweet about how he's an even crueler master than his father somehow fails to get the Israelites on board with his fledgling administration, and Israel is plunged into a seventeen-year civil war that permanently splits the kingdom in two. You don't want to hear about all *that*, though. *You* want to know what all this has to do with penises.

So let's take a second to unpack Rehoboam's proclamation. There's that line about replacing his whips with scorpions, which seems a little inefficient, but you do you, Rehoboam. What I'd really like to talk about is that seemingly innocuous line, **"My little finger is thicker than my father's thighs."** As translated, it seems pretty straightforward—"My dad was a strong dude, I'm a stronger dude"—but it's actually about schlongs, because of course it is. You saw the title of this chapter.

Obviously, Rehoboam is employing an anatomical euphemism here. The word Rehoboam uses for **"thighs"**—*mothnayim* in Hebrew—can be a general term for the hip or waist area but in this case pretty clearly means "penis."[12] In short,[13] "My little finger is thicker than my dad's trouser snake, so you can

---

12. Ilona N. Rashkow, *Taboo or Not Taboo: Sexuality and Family in the Hebrew Bible* (Minneapolis: Fortress Press, 2000), 78.
13. Heh.

just imagine what *I'm* packing."[14] Clearly, Rehoboam was feeling a little inadequate, and it's hard to blame him, considering Solomon famously had six hundred wives and seven hundred concubines, and—as we saw in chapter 3—wrote an entire poem about how awesome his boner was.

But, like most boner brags, this gambit ends up backfiring on Rehoboam pretty badly. Ten of Israel's twelve tribes say, "Methinks he doth protest too much," stage a rebellion, and eventually manage to score independence under a king named Jeroboam, because—as we all know—the most important part of a rebellion is finding a leader with a silly name that rhymes with the equally silly name of the leader you're rebelling against.

ORIGEN MAY HAVE TRIED TO ALLEGORIZE SONG OF SONGS BUT HE TOOK OTHER PASSAGES WAY TOO LITERALLY

Matthew 19 contains one of Jesus' most cryptic sayings:

> "Not everyone can receive this saying, but only those to whom it is given. For there are **eunuchs who have been so from birth**, and there are eunuchs who have been made eunuchs by men, and there are **eunuchs who have made themselves eunuchs for the sake of the kingdom of heaven**. Let the one who is able to receive this receive it." (verses 11–12)

---

14. Athalya Brenner, *The Intercourse of Knowledge: On Gendering Desire and "Sexuality" in the Hebrew Bible* (Leiden, Netherlands: Brill Publishers, 1997), 37.

The most straightforward interpretation here is that Jesus is officially blessing celibacy (an idea St. Paul would greatly expand on in 1 Corinthians), but that hasn't stopped people from using this passage as an excuse for all sorts of weird behavior—for example, Origen of Alexandria, an early Christian thinker who, according to the historian Eusebius, castrated himself, based specifically on these two verses.[15]

Precious Wedding Memories: A Pile of Two Hundred Foreskins

But you're not here to read about embarrassing politicians bragging about their wieners. (You get enough of that in real life.) You saw the title of this chapter, and you want circumcision, and lots of it. I got you covered.[16] This story contains no fewer than *two hundred* circumcisions, all of them performed on corpses. No, I'm not (only) talking about my weekend plans; this is a charming story from the early years of David (after Goliath; before he was crowned king). It begins, as most mass-murder/mass-corpse-desecration stories do, with a girl:

> Then Saul said to David, "Here is my elder daughter Merab. I will give her to you for a wife. Only be valiant for me and fight the LORD's battles." For Saul thought, **"Let not my hand**

---

15. Eusebius, Church History, 6.8.1.
16. Heh.

be against him, but let the hand of the Philistines be against him." (1 Samuel 18:17)

So, Saul—you remember Saul, right? King over Israel? The guy who hates David and is constantly trying to kill him? Saul is like, "Here, marry my daughter Merab." But it's a trick, you see. *It's a plot to get David killed by the Philistines!* And how will that work? It's simple—Saul makes David promise that if he marries his daughter, he'll keep killing Philistines—*and then the Philistines will kill him instead.*

You may have noticed that (1) David was *already* gleefully killing tons of Philistines, and (2) the Philistines have proven themselves, thus far, really bad at killing David—but, shut up, it's a foolproof plan, just like getting rich by selling essential oils. (Talk to me about becoming a representative today!)

So David marries Merab, and—

But at the time when Merab, Saul's daughter, should have been given to David, **she was given to Adriel the Meholathite** for a wife. (verse 19)

—ha, whoops, looks like Saul forgot she was already engaged to someone else. Easy mistake to make, especially when your every waking thought is consumed with a burning desire to murder your military's MVP.

Time for Operation Murder This Guy by Tricking Him into Marrying My Very Attractive Daughter v. 2.0:

Now Saul's daughter Michal loved David. And they told Saul, and the thing pleased him. Saul thought, **"Let me give her to**

him, that she may be a snare for him and that the hand of the Philistines may be against him." (verses 20–21a)

It seems like there'd be an easier way to distract a guy than repeatedly throwing your hot daughters at him (just buy him a sandwich or something), but what do I know? Anyway, David asks Saul if he wants him to pay a bride-price for this schweet deal, and Saul gets super specific:

Then Saul said, "Thus shall you say to David, 'The king desires no bride-price except **a hundred foreskins of the Philistines**, that he may be avenged of the king's enemies.'" Now Saul thought to make David fall by the hand of the Philistines. (verse 25)

Saul wants David to kill a hundred Philistines in battle[17] and then bring their foreskins to him as trophies. I assume that taking foreskins as battle trophies was, like, a *thing* back then, and not just something Saul made up off the top of his head,[18] because that would be *really* weird if it were the latter. But, of course, Saul's plan backfires:

Before the time had expired, David arose and went, along with his men, and **killed two hundred of the Philistines**. And David **brought their foreskins**, which were given in full

---

17. Come to think of it, Saul never says to kill the Philistines—just to take their foreskins. It's not outside the realm of possibility that God was asking David to sneak into Philistine tents and performing a bit of surreptitious surgery. I'd pay to see that as a wacky frat comedy.

18. Heh.

number to the king, that he might become the king's son-in-law. (verses 26b–27a)

David, as always, proves himself quite the overachiever. Saul, however, is apparently not weirded out by the fact that his daughter's fiancé has been handling twice as many corpse penises as he asked him to, because:

Saul gave him his daughter Michal for a wife. (verse 27b)

So, really, everything works out in the end. David gets a wife, Saul gets an enormous pile of corpse foreskins, and Michal gets . . . I mean, she gets David, whom she apparently wanted, but that was *before* he handled, just, *all* the foreskins, so who knows.

TALKING ABOUT HOW EVE WAS MADE FROM ADAM'S "RIB" ENTIRELY MISSES THE POINT OF THE NARRATIVE, AND SO DOES THIS, BUT AT LEAST IT'S FUNNY

While the modern conception of the garden of Eden narrative depicts Eve being crafted from Adam's rib, the Hebrew word in the passage—*hassela*—is actually better translated "side," and often refers to a protruding append-age. This has led at least a few scholars to speculate that the word is being employed euphemistically, and that Eve was in fact made from Adam's *baculum*, or penis bone.[19]

---

19. Robert Martin, *How We Do It: The Evolution and Future of Human Reproduction* (New York: Basic Books, 2013), 9.

For anyone not super up on mammal anatomy, yes, there *is* such a thing as a penis bone. Humans don't have one (nor do whales, rabbits, or horses), but most male mammals have a retractable bone that aids in penile erection,[20] and *yes*, that *does* mean you can talk about animals *literally getting boners*, but seriously, grow up, you're an embarrassment.

The passage in Genesis, so the argument goes, is, in part, an explanation for why humans don't have a *baculum*—which sort of makes sense, since the average man isn't missing any ribs.

Dinah: Weaponized Circumcision

"Murdering people and then circumcising them is cool and all," you're saying, "but do you happen to have a story where people get circumcised and *then* murdered?" And of course I do, because I would never disappoint you. Here's a charming story about Jacob and his sons from the thirty-fourth chapter of Genesis.

You'll recall, of course, that Jacob was the son of Isaac, the grandson of Abraham, the last major Jewish patriarch, and father to twelve sons, plus at least one daughter. This eventually leads to the whole thing where most of his sons sell their brother Joseph

20. Bruce D. Patterson and Charles S. Thaeler Jr., "The Mammalian Baculum: Hypotheses on the Nature of Bacular Variability," *Journal of Mammalogy* 63, no. 1 (1982): 1–15.

into slavery for being such a Technicolor fashionista,[21] but before all that, their sister Dinah gets raped:

> Now Dinah, the daughter Leah had borne to Jacob, went out to visit the women of the land. When Shechem son of Hamor the Hivite, the ruler of that area, saw her, he took her and **raped her**. (Genesis 34:1–2 NIV)

I'm using the NIV here because the ESV says **"humiliated her,"** which is almost tragically euphemistic, and the KJV is like, **"he defiled her,"** which, come on, guys, way to make a girl feel even worse. As men tend to do, though, Shechem drastically misunderstands the encounter:

> His heart was drawn to Dinah daughter of Jacob; **he loved the young woman** and spoke tenderly to her. And Shechem said to his father Hamor, **"Get me this girl as my wife."** (verses 3–4 NIV)

. . . he said, tipping his fedora.

Hamor says okay, and then visits Jacob to arrange a good old-fashioned shotgun wedding:

> Hamor spoke with them, saying, "The soul of my son Shechem longs for your daughter. **Please give her to him to be his wife."** (verse 8)

---

21. Off topic, but we need to have a Very Serious Conversation about how little sense it makes to describe something in a stage production as "Technicolor." USING THE WORD "TECHNICOLOR" IN A CONTEXT IN WHICH IT MAKES NO SENSE DOES NOT COUNT AS A JOKE, ANDREW LLOYD WEBBER, YOU NO-TALENT HACK. I'm sorry. I'll calm down. I'm okay.

For good measure, he throws in some pretty extravagant promises:

> "**Make marriages with us.** Give your daughters to us, and take our daughters for yourselves. **You shall dwell with us**, and the land shall be open to you. Dwell and trade in it, and get property in it." (verses 9–10)

At first, Jacob's sons seem open to the idea of merging the two tribes—that is, as long as Shechem puts his money where his mouth is (so to speak) and goes along with this whole "circumcision" thing that God gave their great-grandpops:

> "Only on this condition will we agree with you—**that you will become as we are by every male among you being circumcised**. Then we will give our daughters to you, and we will take your daughters to ourselves, and we will dwell with you and become one people." (verses 15–16)

Fair enough, figures Shechem. If he's going to be slipping it to Dinah habitually, the least he can do is make sure "it" is kosher. (The *most* he could have done would have been to not rape her in the first place, but, well, hindsight is always twenty-twenty.) He and his dad are so up for being circumcised (so to speak) that they let Jacob's sons do it to them right then and there, and then hobble off to tell their entire tribe about this new penis-modification surgery that all the cool kids are getting:

> "Only on this condition will the men agree to dwell with us to become one people—when every male among us is

circumcised as they are circumcised. **Will not their live-stock, their property and all their beasts be ours?** Only let us agree with them, and they will dwell with us." (verses 22–23)

Slice up your dong, get free stuff! It's a foolproof plan that could not possibly go wrong in any way. Everyone in their city is so hyped about the idea that they have themselves a big penis parade:

And **all who went out of the gate of his city** listened to Hamor and his son Shechem, and **every male was circumcised**, all who went out of the gate of his city. (verse 24)

Part of me is glad for the janitors in the city that they went outside before getting it done; part of me is horrified for whoever happened to be walking by the city at the time. But you're smart, so you've probably figured out by now that this whole plan wasn't *really* about circumcision and the merging of two tribes into one Voltron-esque ultra-mega-tribe. No, this was the prototype for the friggin' Trojan horse:

On the third day, when they were sore, two of the sons of Jacob, Simeon and Levi, Dinah's brothers, **took their swords and came against the city while it felt secure and killed all the males.** They killed Hamor and his son Shechem with the sword and took Dinah out of Shechem's house and went away. (verses 25–26)

Wait, wait, they're murdering every single male in the city? That seems awfully harsh, considering only one of those males raped their sister. Why would they need to kill *all* of them?

> The sons of Jacob came upon the slain and **plundered the city**, because they had defiled their sister. **They took their flocks and their herds, their donkeys, and whatever was in the city and in the field.** All their wealth, all their little ones and their wives, all that was in the houses, they captured and plundered. (verses 27–29)

Oh, I see.

So that worked out pretty well for Jacob's sons, I guess, but the denouement to this narrative is that they end up having to move their camp, because all their neighbors hear about the whole "surprise mass murder" thing and (understandably) worry that something similar might happen to them. Jacob is like, "Guys, did you have to kill *everyone*?"

> Then Jacob said to Simeon and Levi, "You have brought trouble on me by making me stink to the inhabitants of the land, the Canaanites and the Perizzites. My numbers are few, and **if they gather themselves against me and attack me, I shall be destroyed**, both I and my household." **But they said, "Should he treat our sister like a prostitute?"** (verses 30–31)

Because, *obviously*, there were only two choices here. Either (a) let the guy rape their sister, or (b) murder and loot an *entire city*. There is no third option, ever.

WE NEED TO TALK ABOUT EJACULATION FOR A SEC

In the law of Moses, ejaculation is a *big deal*, and not necessarily in a good way:

> "If a man has an emission of semen, he shall bathe his whole body in water and **be unclean until the evening**. And every garment and every skin on which the semen comes shall be washed with water and be unclean until the evening. **If a man lies with a woman and has an emission of semen, both of them shall bathe themselves in water** and be unclean until the evening." (Leviticus 15:16–18)

It's probably worth pointing out that "unclean" in this context only means "unfit to enter the temple." So it's not that sex is "dirty" per se, just that it's an act kept separate from worship.

Then again, maybe the whole thing is just an excuse to brag all day about how you had sex that morning.

St. Paul to the Galatians: "Take Your Wieners . . . Please"

As much fun as it was to circumcise dudes and then murder them, though, it was inevitable that the fun eventually had to come to an end. As the New Testament dawns, a whole new Jewish sect—most people call it "Christianity" these days—is born, and soon hundreds if not thousands of Gentiles are looking to join up. From the start, though, there was, of course, controversy. Were these Gentiles converting to Judaism, or was Christianity a whole new thing? Should Gentile converts be expected to follow the whole law of Moses? More to the point, did they need to get the ol' frankfurter sliced?

In the fifteenth chapter of the book of Acts, the apostles actually hold a big council to make an official proclamation on this, and they come back with "Uh . . . *no*, thanks":

> Therefore my judgment is that **we should not trouble** those of the Gentiles who turn to God, but should write to them to abstain from the things polluted by idols, and from sexual immorality, and from what has been strangled, and from blood. (Acts 15:19–20)

So there's general agreement among the apostles that those who convert to the Christian faith don't have to worry so much about Moses' law, as long as they avoid sleeping around and try to eat right. And yes, their penises, if they have them, stay Gentile. And actually, in his letter to the Colossians, St. Paul goes so far as to say that Christian baptism is the replacement for circumcision:

> In him also you were circumcised with **a circumcision made without hands**, by putting off the body of the flesh, by the circumcision of Christ, **having been buried with him in baptism**, in which you were also raised with him through faith in the powerful working of God, who raised him from the dead. (Colossians 2:11–12)

So that's pretty straightforward. Forget circumcision; baptism is the new hotness.

Except, obviously, it was never quite that cut and dried. (See what I did there?) No matter how many times the apostles announced this decision, there was always someone around trying to talk Christians into getting circumcised—right up until the present day. (That's not an exaggeration; if you look hard enough, you can find plenty of Christian sects that still insist on circumcision.[22])

Paul's letter to the Galatians actually deals directly with this phenomenon. In it, Paul goes through the long list of reasons the Mosaic law doesn't apply to Christians, but it climaxes,[23] arguably, in the fifth chapter:

> Look: I, Paul, say to you that if you accept circumcision, Christ will be of no advantage to you. (Galatians 5:2)

A few verses later, he decides to drive the point home even harder[24]:

> I would they **were even cut off** which trouble you. (verse 12 KJV)

And if you're thinking, "Wait did he just—?" the answer is yes.[25] There's a surface-level sentiment here that Paul wishes these guys preaching circumcision would cut themselves off from the

---

22. The Ethiopian Orthodox Tewahedo Church is one example here. I don't want to rag on those guys, since they're one of the oldest Christian churches in the world, but they do practice circumcision.

23. Heh.

24. Heh.

25. Philip F. Esler, "Group Boundaries and Intergroup Conflict in Galatians: A New Reading of Gal. 5:13–6:10," in *Ethnicity and the Bible*, ed. Mark G. Brett (Boston, MA: Brill Academic Publishers, Inc., 2002), 215–38.

church, but there's also a very wink-wink, nudge-nudge implication that, if these guys like whacking weenies so much, they really ought to just finish the job and take themselves out of the gene pool. Some scholars have argued that, by referencing castration, Paul is trying to draw a line from these circumcision evangelists to several pagan sects of the day whose priests practiced self-emasculation,[26] but in either case, the point remains the same: circumcision was great and all (sort of, I guess), but there's a new covenant now. The old has gone, the new has come; stop thinking about your penises so much, and think about Jesus.

Easier said than done, but still.

---

26. James R. Edwards, "Galatians 5:12," *Novum Testamentum* 53, no. 4 (2011): 319–37.

CHAPTER SIX

MEDIUM-SIZED PIMPIN'

The Many Adventures of Biblical Prostitutes

People who have never read the Bible are often surprised the first time they pick it up at just *how many prostitutes* there are in it. "Um," these hypothetical people will say, "isn't the Bible *against* prostitution?" And the answer, of course, is "Uh . . . yes . . . no . . . it's complicated."

The Mosaic law explicitly forbids *temple* prostitution,[1] which was an interesting thing where you would go to your local temple and pay a fee to have sex with the priest or priestess.[2] (Say what you will, but as a church fundraiser, it beats basement bingo.) *Presumably*, the Ten Commandments' ban on adultery would forbid all other forms of prostitution as well—and most

---

1. See Deuteronomy 23:17.
2. Stephanie L. Budin, "Sacred Prostitution in the First Person," in *Prostitutes and Courtesans in the Ancient World*, ed. Christopher A. Faraone and Laura K. McClure (Madison, WI: University of Wisconsin Press, 2006), 77–94.

ancient Jewish writings support that interpretation[3]—but the Old Testament never really goes out of its way to say so in as many words.

And if the Jewish record on this stuff is a bit ambiguous, the Christian record is *extremely* spotty. A fair number of Christian thinkers—including heavy hitters like Augustine of Hippo[4] and Thomas Aquinas[5]—argued that prostitution was something of a necessary evil, since having it available might prevent worse sins, like rape and marital infidelity. (Seems like a bit of a stretch to me, but there it is.) In medieval Europe, it wasn't entirely unheard of for bishops or other clerics to own brothels, or at least profit from them,[6] and of course they were a great place for "celibate" clergy to blow off some steam. Fortunately, Protestants brought back married clergy and ended this nonsense once and for all, unless you count the endless parade of Protestant pastors who have been caught with prostitutes.

In any case, prostitution is one of those things that peskily continues to exist, no matter how seriously (or unseriously) the Abrahamic faiths oppose it, sort of like divorce, or murder, or literally anything people do. And as long as there are men (or women) desperate for sex and women (or men) desperate for money, it will likely continue to be a thing. Love it or hate it, it's hard to throw a rock without hitting a guy who's solicited a prostitute, which will come in handy if stoning ever comes back *en vogue.*

---

3. E.g., see Babylonian Talmud, Mo'ed Katan 17a.
4. On Order lib. ii. c. 12.
5. Summa Theologica 2–2.10.11.
6. Ruth Mazo Karras, "The Regulation of Brothels in Late Medieval England," *Signs: Journal of Women in Culture and Society* 14, no. 2 (1989): 399–433.

And presumably, that's why the Bible is so casual about it. More than a few passages of Scripture—frequently even the ones about guys you've seen depicted in stained-glass windows—open with "And so, he visited the local prostitute . . ." The text only occasionally pauses to condemn the choice, possibly because of the patriarchal culture of the time, and possibly because if it *did*, you'd just roll your eyes at it like it was your dad lecturing you about your curfew (and/or your habit of soliciting prostitutes). But however you want to take it, the fact remains: if you like prostitutes, you'll love the Bible.

Hosea's Slutty Wife

Hosea's prophecy, like most biblical prophecy, is primarily concerned with how Israel is *just the worst* and God is going to *super* destroy them. To help them understand why, God opens with a metaphor about as subtle as a sledgehammer:

> When the LORD first spoke through Hosea, the LORD said to Hosea, "**Go, take to yourself a wife of whoredom** and have children of whoredom, for the land commits great whoredom by forsaking the LORD." (Hosea 1:2)

Most translations render this as **"Go and marry a prostitute,"** but I'm sticking with the ESV's **"wife of whoredom"** because it sounds like a Megadeth song. Either way, the point is that Israel has been slutty (metaphorically) by worshiping other gods, so Hosea needs to marry a woman who's slutty (literally) to show the Israelites what they're putting God through. Really not a bad plan—sprinkle some awkward marital counseling on top, and you've got yourself a quality idea for a sitcom.

So Hosea finds a prostitute named Gomer, probably he's a big *The Andy Griffith Show* fan, and by the third verse they're popping out kids. Then the new parents start giving the kids names guaranteed to get them beaten up at school:

> She conceived again and bore a daughter. And the LORD said to him, "**Call her name No Mercy**, for I will no more have mercy on the house of Israel, to forgive them at all." (verse 6)

Harsh, right? It gets worse:

> When she had weaned No Mercy, she conceived and bore a son. And the LORD said, "**Call his name Not My People**, for you are not my people, and I am not your God." (verses 8–9)

You might take that last one to mean God is 10,000 percent done with Israel, but he starts walking it back in the next verse, and, in fact, that was the whole point of the "marry a prostitute" thing. There's a reason Hosea *marries* her instead of just hiring her for a weekend and buying her some clothes in a wacky montage:

> Yet the number of the children of Israel shall be like the sand of the sea, which cannot be measured or numbered. And in the place where it was said to them, "You are not my people," **it shall be said to them, "Children of the living God."** (verse 10)

What follows is a chapter-length marriage proposal from God to Israel (cute!), and then the prostitute-marrying hijinks recommence:

And the Lord said to me, "**Go again, love a woman who is loved by another man and is an adulteress**, even as the Lord loves the children of Israel, though they turn to other gods and **love cakes of raisins**." (3:1)

. . . thus confirming that, while prostitution and idolatry might be bad, the real crime is **loving raisins**,[7] which we all know are only good for singing Motown and ruining cookies.

ON BEING AN INFLUENCER, THE STRUGGLES OF

In Isaiah 23, God threatens the Lebanese city of Tyre with destruction:

In that day Tyre will be forgotten for seventy years, like the days of one king. At the end of seventy years, it will happen to Tyre as in **the song of the prostitute**:

"Take a harp;
    go about the city,
    O forgotten prostitute!
Make sweet melody;
    sing many songs,
    that you may be remembered." (verses 15–16)

---

7. If you want the serious explanation for this, it appears that cakes of raisins were either associated with prostitution, or idol worship, or both. No one is really sure. It's a pretty obscure reference.

> Apparently, it was a thing for prostitutes to try to extend their fifteen minutes by pursuing a music career, so basically nothing has changed since the Old Testament.

Onan and Tamar: The Money Shot

You're not here just for prophecies about prostitutes, though—you want the really seedy stuff.[8] Well, good news: I've got something from Genesis that would make even your mom blush. It starts when Jacob's son Judah finds *his* son Er a wife:

> And Judah took a wife for Er his firstborn, and **her name was Tamar**. (Genesis 38:6)

Did you catch that name? When a woman in the Bible is named **Tamar**, it's pretty much always telegraphing, "This woman is about to get sexually abused!"[9] So, you've been warned. Before that can happen, though, this does:

> But Er, Judah's firstborn, was wicked in the sight of the LORD, and **the LORD put him to death**. (verse 7)

Plenty of YouTube atheists have openly blasphemed and lived

---

8. Heh.
9. My parents actually named my sister Tamar. No idea what they were thinking, beyond "We like biblical names" and "The world absolutely does not need another Rachel or Sarah."

to tell the tale,[10] but Er was evidently horrible enough that God had to personally murder him. If you're familiar with the ancient world, you'll know that, for women, few things sucked more than having a husband murdered. But you might also remember from chapter 2 that there was a solution to this problem: a *goel*, or kinsman-redeemer. If your husband died before he could give you a son, it was his closest male relative's duty to marry you and finish the job—which is what Judah asks his second son, Onan, to do.

Now a lot of guys would respond to this charge with, "Cool, free wife, plus some obligatory sex," but Onan's response is more along the lines of "Daaaaaaddddd, I don't waaaaannnnaaaa":

> But Onan knew that the offspring would not be his. So whenever he went in to his brother's wife **he would waste the semen on the ground**, so as not to give offspring to his brother. (verse 9)

He's cool with obligatory intercourse, but since the resulting kids would be credited to his dead brother, he decides to essentially use Tamar as a sex doll. Anyway, now you know where "Onanism," that old-timey word for masturbation, comes from. But while this passage has frequently been cited as condemning autoeroticism,[11] in context, it should be clear that what's being condemned is Onan's refusal to provide Tamar with an heir, not

---

10. Back when the internet was still young, in 2006, there was something called the "Blasphemy Challenge," where atheists were supposed to go on YouTube and openly declare that they denied the Holy Spirit (see Mark 3:29). This got a fair amount of attention, because back in 2006 there was nothing worth watching on YouTube.

11. Arthur J. Mielke, *Christians, Feminists, and the Culture of Pornography* (Lanham, MD: University Press of America, 2002), 59.

masturbation per se.[12] Leave it to male clergy to take a passage about how women aren't cheap sex toys and use it to conclude that man juice is sacred.[13]

Either way, though, God is *super* not cool with what Onan is up to, so:

> And what he did was wicked in the sight of the LORD, and **he put him to death also**. (verse 10)

So that's a body count of two for God in this story so far. Judah's got one more son, but unfortunately for Tamar, he's pre-pubescent, and therefore unlikely to be much help in her quest to get pregnant:

> Then Judah said to Tamar his daughter-in-law, "Remain a widow in your father's house, **till Shelah my son grows up**"— for **he feared that he would die, like his brothers**. (verse 11)

. . . which, I mean, I'd be starting to take the hint there as well.[14]

Shelah eventually reaches adulthood, but then "forgets" to marry her, probably because he doesn't have a death wish. This

---

12. Also, strictly speaking, Onan isn't *masturbating*.

13. You can probably build a case against masturbation through a broader reading of Scripture. (Jesus condemns lust in Matthew 5:28, and if you can masturbate without thinking lustful thoughts, you're more talented than most.) That said, though, if you're the sort of person who spends a lot of time wondering if masturbation is a sin, you should probably get a hobby, for more reasons than one.

14. Actually, how great would it be if Tamar was actually the one murdering her husbands and then telling everyone, "Uh, God did it," and her husbands were so completely awful that people were like, "Yeah, that checks out"? Someone get Anita Diamant or somebody to write that novel.

leaves Tamar even more desperate than before (which is saying something), but then she learns that her double-ex-father-in-law is passing through her neck of the woods, so:

> And when Tamar was told, "Your father-in-law is going up to Timnah to shear his sheep," **she took off her widow's garments** and covered herself with a veil, wrapping herself up, **and sat at the entrance to Enaim** which is on the road to Timnah. (verses 13–14a)

It's hard to tell exactly what Tamar's desired outcome for this encounter is, but Judah knows what *he* wants out of it:

> When Judah saw her, **he thought she was a prostitute**, for she had covered her face. (verse 15)

It makes sense that the guy who raised two sons *literally so awful God had to personally murder them* would be such a class act himself.

In fairness to Judah, he's on this little excursion mainly to take his mind off the fact that his wife just died, so you can kind of understand why he's seeing prostitutes everywhere he looks. Still, you'd think being widowed *once* would give him some empathy for someone who's been widowed *twice*, but you'd be wrong:

> He turned to her at the roadside and said, **"Come, let me come in to you,"** for he did not know that she was his daughter-in-law. She said, "What will you give me, that you may come in to me?" (verse 16)

So it takes Tamar less than a second to flip the switch from "grieving widow" to "opportunistic hooker." Judah tells her he'll pay her a whole goat, because goats were the Bitcoin of the ancient world; he doesn't actually have one with him, but he's good for it, he swears. She asks for his staff and signet ring as collateral, and they do the deed.

Judah spends three months unsuccessfully trying to find that hooker who wants his goat, but then:

About three months later Judah was told, "**Tamar your daughter-in-law has been immoral.** Moreover, she is pregnant by immorality." And Judah said, "**Bring her out, and let her be burned.**" (verse 24)

There it is, folks: men who have been widowed are cool to blow off some steam, but women who have been widowed *twice* get burned at the stake for sleeping around. I don't know about you, but double standards like that really get my goat. (Eh? Eh? Get it? It is a joke.) In any case, Tamar is just about *done* with this crap:

As she was being brought out, she sent word to her father-in-law, "**By the man to whom these belong, I am pregnant.**" And she said, "Please identify whose these are, **the signet and the cord and the staff.**" (verse 25)

Judah says, "Welp, you got me":

Then Judah identified them and said, "**She is more righteous than I,** since I did not give her to my son Shelah." **And he did not know her again.** (verse 26)

So the *only* thing Judah thinks he did wrong was fail to give Tamar another terrible son to marry. Not raising a bunch of tool bags for sons in the first place; not trying to murder his daughter-in-law for doing something he was more than happy to do himself; not trying to pass off a goat as a fair payment for sex—the *only* thing he did wrong here, in his mind, was fail to ruin Tamar's life a third time.

So everyone comes out of this story either dead or widowed and having learned nothing. Really, the only one who gets a happy ending (so to speak) is the goat, since he managed to stay out of the whole mess.

ON WEIRD SEXUAL METAPHYSICS, PAUL'S

In his first epistle to the Corinthians, St. Paul is pretty upset about the parishioners' habit of soliciting prostitutes:

> Do you not know that your bodies are members of Christ? **Shall I then take the members of Christ and make them members of a prostitute?** Never! Or do you not know that **he who is joined to a prostitute becomes one body with her**? For, as it is written, "The two will become one flesh." (6:15–16)

So if you've ever had sex with someone, you're *literally sharing a body with them right now*. Someone make that horror movie, please.

Rahab: Did Prostitutes Not Have Doors, Or . . . ?

Between the Torah and the book of Judges, you'll find one of the Bible's most controversial books. While Moses' books narrate everything from the beginning of the world up to Israel's trek to the promised land, the book of Joshua tells the story of the promised land's conquest. It's controversial for two reasons: first, because certain people aren't cool with Israel just randomly showing up in Canaan and murdering everyone (for *some* reason), and second, because it turns out there's not a lot of historical evidence for the events it describes.[15] You'd *think* that second point would mitigate problems with the first for the naysayers, but nah.[16]

But even if you find the book morally repugnant and historically questionable, it still has its moments. (It's sort of like the History Channel that way.) It's full of covert ops, bloody battles, and also that part where Joshua fights the battle of Jericho (Jericho, JerichoOoOoOoOo) and the walls come a-tumbling down. And also, there's a prostitute, which is why I'm bringing it up right now.

This particular narrative happens just before the whole Jericho (JerichoOoOoOoOo) thing, and finds Israel encamped at Shittim (it means "acacia trees," *you child*), trying to plan their attack. Joshua sends in a couple of spies to do some reconnaissance:

---

15. G. W. Ahlström, "Another Moses Tradition," *Journal of Near Eastern Studies* 39, no. 1 (1980): 65–69.

16. It's also worth repeating the old maxim that absence of evidence is not evidence of absence. A lack of historical evidence for Joshua doesn't necessarily mean nothing in the book happened; it may mean that we simply misunderstand the evidence in front of us, or just that the author of Joshua wasn't overly concerned with literal historical precision. At the very least, the author seems to be highly given to hyperbole, frequently reporting that Israel "totally destroyed" tribes that show up again just a couple of chapters later.

And Joshua the son of Nun sent two men secretly from Shittim as spies, saying, "Go, view the land, especially Jericho." And they went and came into the house of a **prostitute** whose name was Rahab and **lodged there**. (Joshua 2:1)

Yes, **"lodged there"** is quite possibly a euphemism for making use of the prostitute Rahab's services—because, if we learned nothing else from James Bond movies, we learned that the main part of being a spy is just having *stupid* amounts of sex. The Hebrew verb here is *wayiskabu*, "to lie down," with all the usual implications.

That's not the *only* thing it could mean, though. First-century historian Josephus refers to Rahab as simply an "innkeeper,"[17] and it wasn't uncommon at the time for brothels and inns to be one and the same.[18] One way or another, though, Rahab's place was clearly a great place to spend a night—at least until the Shittim hit the fan:

And it was told to the king of Jericho, "Behold, men of Israel have come here tonight to search out the land." Then the king of Jericho sent to Rahab, saying, "**Bring out the men who have come to you**, who entered your house, for they have come to search out all the land." (verses 2–3)

So now the cops are banging on the door—a lousy way to end a trip to the local whorehouse, to be sure, but arguably worse if you're there as spies from an invading army. Fortunately, Rahab

---

17. Josephus, Antiquities 5.8.
18. Robert G. Boling and G. Ernest Wright, *Joshua: A New Translation with Notes and Commentary* (New Haven, CT: Yale University Press, 1995), 145.

knows how to take care of her clientèle—she hides them and lies like a rug:

> But the woman had taken the two men and hidden them. And she said, "True, the men came to me, but I did not know where they were from. And when the gate was about to be closed at dark, the men went out. **I do not know where the men went.** Pursue them quickly, for you will overtake them." (verses 4–5)

They buy it and run out the city gates, chasing some imaginary spies toward the Jordan River and basically looking like chumps. Then Rahab tells the actual spies that she knows God is on their side because she heard about that whole "parting the Red Sea" thing and also it would be super cool if they would let her live when they invaded, since she just saved their butts and all. The spies think that sounds okay. And then

> **she let them down by a rope through the window**, for her house was built into the city wall, so that **she lived in the wall.** (verse 15)

And if right now you're saying, "Wait, **she *lived* in the wall???**" just know that it's Joshua burying the lede here, not me. Apparently, this was a thing in the ancient world[19]—you would build your home into the city wall, which might come in handy if you ever had spies to sneak out, but would also be a bit of a problem if the walls ever came a-tumbling down.

Things work out pretty well for Rahab, though—the invading

---

19. David Merling, "Rahab: The Woman Who Fulfilled the Word of Yhwh," *Andrews University Seminary Studies* 41, no. 1 (2003): 31–44.

armies make good on the promise not to murder her. Then she settles with them in the promised land, and—according to Matthew 1:5—becomes an ancestor of King David, and, eventually, Jesus. So, in ancient Jericho, as in '80s rom-coms, being a hooker with a heart of gold pays off.

THE THIRD OR FOURTH MOST HORRIFYING THING ABOUT SOLOMON'S BABY-CHOPPING PLAN

Most people know the story of how King Solomon solves a dispute over a baby by offering to cut it in half. (Spoiler: the child's actual mother cries out in protest, while the other doesn't, because, in addition to being a liar and a kidnapper, she is apparently also a sociopath.) It's one of those go-to stories for Sunday school, because, as Roald Dahl taught us, nothing is more appropriate for children than stories about murdering children.

What often gets lost in the Sunday-school-ification of the narrative, though, is how the women knew each other:

Then **two prostitutes** came to the king and stood before him. (1 Kings 3:16)

One wonders if having babies around the brothel was bad for business. Or—who knows—maybe it was *good* for business. Who doesn't love babies?

I mean, aside from that second prostitute.

And Speaking of Weird Ways to Leave Hookers' Places: We Need to Have a Very Serious Talk About Just How Extra Samson Was

If you've never picked up a Bible, you probably think of Samson as the Old Testament version of Hercules—and you're more right than you realize. But he's not the version of Hercules you find in Disney cartoons or syndicated television; he's the one you find in the original Greek myths—a bumbling musclehead who occasionally wants to do the right thing but usually just exists as a tool for deities to pull off wacky pranks on mortals with. Samson is one of the titular figures in the book of Judges, which is to say that he repeatedly delivers Israel from foreign oppressors, but mostly in ridiculous ways, like tying foxes' tails together and lighting them on fire. (No, really—see Judges 15:4.) Some of his other hijinks include murdering a thousand guys armed only with a donkey's jawbone (verse 16) and tearing a lion apart with his bare hands (14:6)—and then making up a stupid riddle about the whole thing, like he's Will-freaking-Shortz.

What we need to talk about right now, though—this being the chapter about prostitutes and all—is Samson's appreciation for fine hookers. In Judges 16, Samson is between one failed marriage and one failed cohabitation (his famous fling with Delilah), and so:

> Samson went to Gaza, and there **he saw a prostitute, and he went in to her**. (verse 1)

Samson, as we've said, is a walking bag of meat who thinks mainly with his biceps and his crotch, so **"he saw a prostitute"** is

152

really all the explanation we need for **"he went in to her."** Sex was just the guy's Achilles' heel, which—I mean, "sexual addiction" is a much more believable tragic flaw than "like, he's invincible, except for his heel, and if he gets hit in the heel, he dies." (*The Iliad* was clearly written by a six-year-old boy playing with action figures.)

In any case, his sexual habits, like any good Achilles' heel, get him into trouble:

> The Gazites were told, "Samson has come here." And **they surrounded the place and set an ambush for him all night at the gate of the city**. They kept quiet all night, saying, "Let us wait till the light of the morning; then we will kill him." (verse 2)

Spending the night in a city full of people who want to kill you is rarely a good idea, but if you're sufficiently *awesome*, you don't need good ideas. Samson, as it happens, *is* awesome, which means that his crotch rarely writes a check his biceps can't cash:

> But Samson lay till midnight, and at midnight he arose and **took hold of the doors of the gate of the city and the two posts, and pulled them up, bar and all**, and put them on his shoulders and carried them to the top of the hill that is in front of Hebron. (verse 3)

In case you're skimming: *he literally just rips the city gates off their hinges and leaves with them*, then chucks them at the top of a hill forty miles away, like a big showoff. The gates, you'll remember, were the exact place the Gazites were waiting to ambush him, and they apparently made no attempt to follow through. You tell me, though—if the guy you're lying in wait for rips two five-ton gates off their hinges right in front of you, are *you* going to do anything about it? I'd just rush home to wash my pants and then hit the gym for a few extra reps.

I WANT TO PARTY WITH BABYLON

Revelation 17 describes (literally) the biggest whore in the whole Bible:

> **I saw a woman sitting on a scarlet beast** that was full of blasphemous names, and it had seven heads and ten horns. The woman was arrayed in purple and scarlet, and adorned with gold and jewels and pearls, holding in her hand a golden cup full of abominations and the impurities of her sexual immorality. And on her forehead was written a name of mystery: **"Babylon the great, mother of prostitutes and of earth's abominations."** And I saw the woman, drunk with the blood of the saints, the blood of the martyrs of Jesus. (verses 3b–6a)

The most straightforward interpretation here is that the so-called Whore of Babylon probably represents the Roman Empire and its proclivity for persecuting Christians, but that hasn't stopped people throughout history from speculating wildly about what else she could possibly represent. Martin Luther, for instance, famously adorned his German translation of Revelation with woodcuts that explicitly depicted the Whore as the Catholic Church.[20]

Saul to Jonathan: "Your Mom Is a Whore"

Clearly, there are a lot of whores in the Bible. That hasn't stopped people from trying to bowdlerize them out, though. For one example, let's take a look at a charming anecdote about King Saul and his son Jonathan.

I touched on Saul's never-ending quest to make David, his eventual successor, super dead in the previous chapters, so I won't belabor it here. When this story begins, David has been hanging around Saul's court for a while, partly because he's the best soldier in Saul's army, and partly because Saul has hired him to play him lullabies every night. He's also become besties with Saul's son Jonathan, who by now has figured out that David is likely to succeed Saul instead of him, but he's cool with it because it will give him time to pursue his true calling as an Instagram influencer or whatever.

Anyway, Jonathan notices that Dad is getting even more stabby than usual and warns David to run for the hills. A few days pass, and Saul is like, "Hmm, I haven't seen that David kid in a while":

But on the second day, the day after the new moon, David's place was empty. And Saul said to Jonathan his son, "Why

---

20. Roland Herbert Bainton, *Here I Stand: A Life of Martin Luther* (Nashville: Abingdon Press, 2013), 343.

has not the son of Jesse come to the meal, **either yesterday or today?**" (1 Samuel 20:27)

You'd think it wouldn't be *that* hard to say "He got tired of you trying to murder him," but Jonathan knows how his dad can be, so he tries the ol' "He's at church camp" excuse:

Jonathan answered Saul, "David earnestly asked leave of me to go to Bethlehem. **He said, 'Let me go, for our clan holds a sacrifice in the city**, and my brother has commanded me to be there. So now, if I have found favor in your eyes, let me get away and see my brothers.' For this reason he has not come to the king's table." (verses 28–29)

Saul, however, is having none of it:

Then Saul's anger was kindled against Jonathan, and he said to him, "**You son of a perverse, rebellious woman**, do I not know that you have chosen the son of Jesse to your own shame, and to **the shame of your mother's nakedness?**" (verse 30)

Thanks to censorious translation, we have an enraged Saul calling Jonathan a **"son of a perverse, rebellious woman,"** which is something no actual enraged person has ever said. The New Living Translation renders the line **"stupid son of a whore,"** which is a *little* better, but still sounds like dialogue your mom would write for the bad guys in a church pageant.

In any case, Saul appears to be spontaneously inventing the storied "mother insult" here, which I admit is an insult genre that never made a whole lot of sense to me. If you're going after a guy's mother, isn't that just a tacit admission that you can't think of anything insulting to say about *him*? And in Saul's case, Jonathan's (perverse, rebellious) mother is also Saul's (perverse, rebellious) wife, so if the "I am rubber, you are glue" doctrine ever applied anywhere, this is it.

Had I been in Jonathan's place, I would have brought up some of these Very Serious Concerns, but what happens next suggests that doing so would have been a Very Bad Idea:

> **Then Saul hurled his spear at him to strike him down**; so Jonathan knew that his father had decided to put David to death. (verse 33 NASB)

Fortunately, the spear misses, because, if there's anything we've learned about Saul, it's that he's absolute garbage at killing people.

IT'S SORT OF LIKE "MALE MODEL" OR "MALE NURSE"

Most of this chapter has focused on female prostitutes, because, well, there's a lot more of them, in the Bible as in life,[21] but I didn't forget the dudes either:

> . . . and there were also **male cult prostitutes** in the land. (1 Kings 14:24a)

---

21. It's estimated that 80 percent of the world's prostitutes are female. See Patti Feureisen, *Invisible Girls: The Truth about Sexual Abuse* (New York: Basic Books, 2018), 245.

That's basically it. The Bible's like, "Yup, male prostitutes are a thing too. Thanks for reading!"

Oholah, Oholibah, and a Whole Lot of Donkey Penises

At the beginning of this chapter, we talked briefly about how Hosea used prostitution as a handy metaphor for idol worship. Ezekiel, who lived about two hundred years after Hosea,[22] returns to that same well and then *drinks it dry*, repeatedly delving into lengthy, graphic descriptions of prostitutes doing what prostitutes do, like he's some sort of '90s rapper who just found out about your mom. The first of them climaxes with this far-from-subtle bit:

> "You also took your fine jewelry—including my gold and my silver that I had given you. Then you **made for yourself male images and had sex with them!**" (Ezekiel 16:17 isv)

. . . which, as far as I know, is the only mention of dildos in the Bible, and you just got to read it, so yay?

Ezekiel's most infamous passage, though, is a story of two sisters:

> "Son of man, there were two women, the daughters of one mother. They played the whore in Egypt; they played the whore in their youth; **there their breasts were pressed and their virgin bosoms handled.**" (23:2–3)

---

22. Moshe Greenberg, *Ezekiel, 1–20: A New Translation with Introduction and Commentary* (New Haven, CT: Yale University Press, 1983), 10.

You can tell Ezekiel's book was written by a man, for men, from the fact that he apparently thinks that the height of female sexual pleasure is getting your breasts honked. God goes on to identify these two charming ladies as "Oholah" and "Oholibah,"[23] who respectively represent the kingdoms of Israel and Judah.[24] After rescuing them from Egypt, God marries them both, which technically violates the ban on marrying two sisters in Leviticus 18:18, but it's just an analogy, so try to keep up.

By the time of Ezekiel's composition, Israel had already been destroyed by invaders, so God says Oholah was killed by her various illicit lovers. Oholibah, however, learned nothing from that eventuality:

> "Her sister Oholibah saw this, and **she became more corrupt than her sister in her lust and in her whoring**, which was worse than that of her sister." (verse 11)

I'm sure you're hoping for a graphic description of Oholibah's **whoring**, right? No? Too bad:

> "Yet she increased her whoring, remembering the days of her youth, when she played the whore in the land of Egypt and lusted after her lovers there, **whose members were like those of donkeys, and whose issue was like that of horses**." (verses 19–20)

---

23. These names do have meanings, but nothing all that interesting: they mean something like "her tent" and "my tent is in her," respectively.
24. Judah is the small nation that broke off from Israel after Rehoboam's fixation on his own penis brought about civil war (see chapter 5).

... which is about as unpleasantly specific as descriptions get. Am I to take it that donkeys have bigger penises, but horses ejaculate more? I have no idea (and now I can't stop thinking about it), but either way, the message is that you can't be a prostitute and expect not to get pimp-slapped:

> Therefore, O Oholibah, thus says the LORD God: "Behold, I will stir up against you your lovers from whom you turned in disgust, and I will bring them against you from every side: . . . I will direct my jealousy against you, that they may deal with you in fury. **They shall cut off your nose and your ears**, and your survivors shall fall by the sword." (verses 22–25b)

If you're wondering why the book of Ezekiel is only barely distinguishable from a *Penthouse* letter,[25] one explanation offered by scholars is the strong influence Babylon was exerting on the Hebrew world at the time. Babylon—which had already destroyed Israel and was in the process of wearing down Judah—was, as a nation, *super* into prostitutes. It was also one where women were afforded quite a few more legal rights than Judahite women, being allowed to own and sell property, inherit wealth from their husbands, and file for divorce.[26] In a sociopolitical milieu like that, you can imagine there would be a ton of male anxiety about prostitutes and unfaithful wives.

Or something like that. I'm not a historian; I'm just a guy looking for excuses to write about donkey penises.

---

25. According to certain traditions, the first-century rabbi Akiva ben Yosef actually taught that Ezekiel should be read only by men over thirty, because no one else could handle it. If you're not a man over thirty, please forget you read this section.

26. Catherine Clark Kroeger and Mary J. Evans, eds., *The IVP Women's Bible Commentary* (Downers Grove, IL: InterVarsity Press, 2002), 397.

CHAPTER SEVEN

IT'S MAGIC!

Seemingly Unnecessary Miracles

In the eighteenth century, Scottish philosopher David Hume published an argument that no claim of a miracle could be reasonably believed.[1] It goes something like this: (1) the best way to understand the universe is through repeated, replicated observation; (2) miracles, by definition, are not repeatable or replicable; (3) therefore, all miracles can be dismissed out of hand. It's a convincing argument, as long as you don't think about it for more than two seconds.

There are actually a lot of problems with Hume's line of thinking, but the worst of them is probably that it's essentially a tautology—if you begin by assuming that empiricism is the only path to truth, *of course* you're going to conclude that empiricism is the only path to truth. All Hume really proved was that miracles are scientifically unverifiable—which, with all due respect to Mr. Hume: *duh*.

---

1. David Hume, *An Enquiry Concerning Human Understanding*, sec. 10.

I'm not sure *why* Hume devoted a not-insignificant chunk of his life to proving what we all already knew about miracles, when there are so many other more interesting things to be said about them: for instance, that they're often really, really *stupid*. Yes, the word "miracle" often refers to a blind man receiving sight or a cripple leaping to his feet and walking, but—according to the Bible, at least—it can also mean an innocent fig tree dying a needless death or a donkey having a Mister Ed moment. I guess they can't all be home runs, but sometimes you wonder why God even bothered.

We'll dive back into more of the sex stuff after this chapter, I promise, but I need to cleanse my palate first, so here are the Bible's top miracles that no one asked for.

Balaam: From the Sublime to the Asinine

Israel's famously fraught relationship with Moab (see chapters 1, 2, and 8) is at a steady simmer when Moses leads them through Moabite territory en route to the promised land in Numbers 22. Balak, the Moabite king, upon seeing the Israelite nation's sheer size, reacts the same way anyone facing such an existential threat would: he hires a wacky magician. Specifically, a guy named Balaam:

> So Balak the son of Zippor, who was king of Moab at that time, sent messengers to Balaam . . . saying, "Behold, a people has come out of Egypt. They cover the face of the earth, and they are dwelling opposite me. **Come now, curse this people for me**, since they are too mighty for me." (Numbers 22:4b–6a)

Balaam says, "Cool, a paying gig that doesn't involve doing card tricks for six-year-olds," packs up his donkey, and starts heading toward Moab. God—being generally pro-Israel—is *not* happy about it and sends his angel to give Balaam a hard time:

> And the donkey saw the angel of the LORD standing in the road, with **a drawn sword in his hand. And the donkey turned aside** out of the road and went into the field. And Balaam struck the donkey, to turn her into the road. (verse 23)

So Balaam's donkey can take a hint, but Balaam can't, and he tries to solve his problems with the only method that has ever existed: violence. He and the donkey work their way through several verses' worth of vaudevillian slapstick:

> And when the donkey saw the angel of the LORD, **she pushed against the wall and pressed Balaam's foot against the wall.** So he struck her again. (verse 25)

Eventually, the angel gets annoyed and kicks things up a notch:

> Then the angel of the LORD went ahead and stood in a narrow place, where there was no way to turn either to the right or to the left. When the donkey saw the angel of the LORD, **she lay down under Balaam.** (verses 26–27a)

. . . wait for it:

> And Balaam's anger was kindled, and **he struck the donkey with his staff.** (verse 27b)

When it becomes clear that Balaam is never going to get a clue, God starts . . . talking out of his ass[2]:

> Then **the LORD opened the mouth of the donkey**, and she said to Balaam, "What have I done to you, that you have struck me these three times?" (verse 28)

Having the donkey speak here isn't an entirely random choice; animals gaining the gift of gab to suggest the presence of deities is a bit of a motif in Near Eastern literature (which also accounts for that talking snake in Genesis, in case that was also still bothering you, Mr. Dawkins)[3]—and, of course, having the ass speak also raises the rather heavy-handed question of who the real "ass" is in this scenario. Balaam, however, continues failing to understand irony:

> And Balaam said to the donkey, "Because you have made a fool of me. **I wish I had a sword in my hand**, for then I would kill you." (verse 29)

. . . which, you'd think that if *anyone* could appreciate what a goldmine a talking donkey is, it would be the starving magician, but *apparently not.* On the other hand, I do know of at least one person who could lend Balaam a sword:

---

2. If you're offended by my choice of words here, keep in mind that "ass" (a donkey) and "ass" (a butt), while homophones (and homographs in American English), are actually etymologically unrelated. So I'm not being vulgar; *you're* the one being vulgar.

3. Michael S. Heiser, *The Unseen Realm: Recovering the Supernatural Worldview of the Bible* (Bellingham, WA: Lexham Press, 2015), 74.

Then **the LORD opened the eyes of Balaam**, and he saw the angel of the LORD standing in the way, with his drawn sword in his hand. **And he bowed down and fell on his face.** (verse 31)

Balaam and the angel proceed to have a little sword-augmented chat, in which Balaam extra-super-pinky-swears to only say the words God gives him permission to. Then he shows up to his Israelite-cursing gig in Moab and proceeds to bless Israel, instead of cursing them, for a solid two chapters.

Punk'd!

ON TEACHING A MAN TO FISH

In the seventeenth chapter of Matthew, the Pharisees demand to know why Jesus hasn't been paying his temple taxes. Jesus' response, at first, seems to be a delightful shrug and an "I'm *God*, I don't have to pay taxes":

> "What do you think, Simon? **From whom do kings of the earth take toll or tax? From their sons or from others?**" And when he said, "From others," Jesus said to him, **"Then the sons are free."** (verses 25b–26)

But then, to hammer home the "I'm God" thing, he literally just squeezes his money out of a dead fish, because he can:

MURDER-BEARS, MOONSHINE, AND MAYHEM

> "However, not to give offense to them, go to the sea
> and cast a hook and **take the first fish that comes up,**
> **and when you open its mouth you will find a shekel.**
> Take that and give it to them for me and for yourself."
> (verse 27)

Jesus Really Doesn't Like Fig Trees

In the twenty-first chapter of St. Matthew's gospel, Jesus is seriously jonesing for some figs:

> And seeing a fig tree by the wayside, he went to it and **found**
> **nothing on it** but only leaves. (verse 19a)

. . . probably because (as the parallel passage in Mark 11 tells us) figs aren't in season right now. Bummer. What's your second-favorite fruit, Jesus?

> And he said to it, "May no fruit ever come from you again!"
> **And the fig tree withered at once.** (verse 19b)

So I'm guessing the life application here is "Don't mess with Jesus when he's hangry."

If it seems unreasonable to expect a fig tree to bear fruit out of season, that's only because you know nothing about fig cultivation, you hack. Before the fruit-bearing season, most fig trees will produce a sort of bland pre-fruit called *breba*,[4] and given the clues from the broader context (Passover is happening, which would make it early spring), it wouldn't have been asking that much to expect the tree to at least have some of *that*.

And, for whatever it's worth, Jesus says the *real* lesson here is about faith:

> When the disciples saw it, they marveled, saying, **"How did the fig tree wither at once?"** And Jesus answered them, "Truly, I say to you, if you have faith and do not doubt, you will not only do what has been done to the fig tree, but even if you say to this mountain, 'Be taken up and thrown into the sea,' it will happen. **And whatever you ask in prayer, you will receive**, if you have faith." (verses 20–22)

. . . which sounds an *awful* lot like an attempt to cover for getting caught doing something silly, but you do you, Jesus.

Both Matthew and Mark apparently thought the fig-murdering story was important enough to include in their gospels; Luke doesn't mention it, but he does include an entirely different fig-murdering story:

> And he told this parable: "A man had a fig tree planted in his vineyard, and he came seeking fruit on it and found none. And he said to the vinedresser, 'Look, for three years now I have come seeking fruit on this fig tree, and I find none. **Cut it down.** Why should it use up the ground?' And he answered

---

4. Z. Yablowitz, G. Nir, and A. Erez, "Breba Fig Production in Israel: Regular and Pesticide-Free Systems," *Acta Hortic* 480, no. 23 (1998): 137–42.

him, 'Sir, let it alone this year also, until I dig around it and put on manure. **Then if it should bear fruit next year, well and good; but if not, you can cut it down.'"** (Luke 13:6–9)

The broader context (see verses 1–5) makes it clear that "fruit" here represents repentance—in other words, this is a story about how you've got a limited time in your life to repent of your sins, so you better get on that. Mark, in his gospel, seems to be making a similar point—he inserts the story of Jesus whipping people in the temple (see chapter 4) into the *middle* of the fig-tree-murdering narrative, apparently to drive home the point that *all* of us, including those running the temple as a for-profit business, get a limited number of chances to turn away from our sin. And that if you're a fig tree, no one is keeping you around just for the ambience.

THIS IS ONE OF THE COOLEST THINGS THAT HAPPENS IN THE ENTIRE BIBLE, AND THEY GIVE IT LITERALLY HALF A VERSE

In the fourth chapter of Daniel, Babylonian king Nebuchadnezzar won't stop boasting about his power and riches, so God decides to humble him by borrowing a trick from party hypnotists:

He was driven from among men and **ate grass like an ox,** and his body was wet with the dew of heaven till **his hair grew as long as eagles' feathers, and his nails were like birds' claws.** (verse 33b)

> Can anyone explain to me why no one's made a
> movie out of this? It would work as almost any genre,
> from wacky comedy to Cronenbergian body horror.
> Someone get on that.

Let's Talk About Jonah, Since Basically Everyone Misses the Point of That One

Even if you've never picked up a Bible, you probably still know the story of Jonah (y'know, the whale guy)—or, at least, you *think* you do. The Sunday school version, though, nearly always cuts out the last chapter—which is where we find out what a massive tool Jonah was. But since this is the "weird miracles" chapter, and "swallowed by a whale and lived to tell about it" is definitely a weird miracle, let's talk about it. It starts out the way you remember:

> Now the word of the LORD came to Jonah the son of Amittai, saying, **"Arise, go to Nineveh**, that great city, and call out against it, for their evil has come up before me." (Jonah 1:1–2)

Nineveh, if you don't know, was basically Rome before Rome was a thing. It was the capital of the then very "it" Assyrian Empire, and it spent a solid half century as the world's biggest city.[5] It's not a backwater ripe for a big tent revival meeting; it's a metropolis any of us would have been nervous to visit—especially if the purpose of the visit was to demand submission to the deity of a tiny

---

5. Stephanie Dalley, "Nineveh after 612 B.C.," *Altorientalische Forschungen* 20, no. 1 (1993): 134–47.

monotheistic sect that barely registered as a blip on their political radar. We'll soon learn that Jonah's reason for refusing the call is a *bit* more complicated than that, but hopefully that information makes his immediate response a little more understandable:

> But Jonah rose to flee to Tarshish from the presence of the Lord. **He went down to Joppa and found a ship going to Tarshish.** So he paid the fare and went down into it, to go with them to Tarshish, away from the presence of the Lord. (verse 3)

You're probably hoping that I'll fill you in with fun tidbits about Tarshish, like I did with Nineveh, but unfortunately, no one currently living knows what a "Tarshish" is.[6] Attempts have been made to connect it with known cities, but "sailed for Tarshish" appears to be the ancient Hebrew equivalent of "took the midnight train going an-y-y-where." God isn't thrilled about Jonah going AWOL, so he comes after him, as is his wont, via the weather:

> But the Lord hurled a great wind upon the sea, and **there was a mighty tempest on the sea**, so that the ship threatened to break up. (verse 4)

The sailors then fumble desperately to save their precious cargo of (I assume) fidget spinners and poop-emoji keychains, while Jonah spends half a dozen verses jumping up and down and yelling that it's his fault and they need to throw him overboard. After asking around about who invited the weirdo, they sigh, roll their eyes, and oblige. You know what's coming next:

---

6. Isidore Singer and M. Seligsohn, "Tarshish," in *Jewish Encyclopedia*, ed. Isidore Singer (Chicago: Funk & Wagnalls, 1906), 12:65.

> And the LORD appointed a **great fish** to swallow up Jonah. And **Jonah was in the belly of the fish three days** and three nights. (verse 17)

Pedants often point out that the passage describes the creature that swallows Jonah as a "great fish," not a whale per se, but the linguistic distinction between whales and fish is a pretty recent one, so it could have easily been either.[7] Then again, there aren't any known species of whales *or* fish anatomically capable of swallowing a man and keeping him alive for three days,[8] so we might actually be talking about some sort of bizarre, inscrutable sea beast—possibly one so horrible that you'll go mad just imagining it.[9]

It turns out there's not a lot to do inside a whale, so Jonah spends the entirety of chapter 2 singing the "I'm Very Sorry" song. God hears it, digs it, and

> the LORD spoke to the fish, and **it vomited Jonah out** upon the dry land. (2:10)

Jonah (hopefully) takes a bath,[10] and then takes the Nineveh gig:

7. John Dupré, "Are Whales Fish?" in *Folkbiology*, ed. Douglas L. Medin and Scott Atran (Cambridge, MA: MIT Press, 1999), 461–75.
8. Rose Eveleth, "Could a Whale Accidentally Swallow You? It Is Possible," *Smithsonian*, February 25, 2013, https://www.smithsonianmag.com/smart-news/could-a-whale-accidentally-swallow-you-it-is-possible-26353362/.
9. (Try it and let me know.)
10. Actually, ambergris, a key ingredient in many expensive perfumes, is extracted from whale vomit. So maybe Jonah comes out of the ordeal literally smelling like a rose.

Jonah began to go into the city, going a day's journey. And he called out, **"Yet forty days, and Nineveh shall be overthrown!"** (3:4)

You might expect a city as large as Nineveh to be more or less accustomed to crazy men who reek of whale hork wandering its streets and shouting things about the apocalypse, but it turns out you'd be wrong:

The word reached the king of Nineveh, and he arose from his throne, removed his robe, **covered himself with sackcloth, and sat in ashes.** (verse 6)

And God has mercy on Nineveh. Happy ending, right? Haha, not for everyone—in fact, Jonah's response is so embarrassing that many modern scholars consider Jonah to be an obvious work of satire[11]:

But it displeased Jonah exceedingly, and he was angry. And he prayed to the LORD and said, "O LORD, is not this what I said when I was yet in my country? **That is why I made haste to flee to Tarshish; for I knew that you are a gracious God and merciful**, slow to anger and abounding in steadfast love, and relenting from disaster." (4:1–2)

In case you're skimming, Jonah says the reason he originally refused to go to Nineveh wasn't fear of the Assyrians, but *because he was worried God would show them mercy.* You might have

---

11. John C. Holbert, "'Deliverance Belongs to Yahweh!' Satire in the Book of Jonah," *Journal for the Study of the Old Testament* 6, no. 21 (1981): 59–81.

noticed that God's habit of showing mercy to people is literally the only reason Jonah is still alive and not currently wending his way through whale intestines, but Jonah doesn't see it that way. He's so upset by Nineveh's failure to turn into a giant smoking crater that—well, see for yourself:

"Therefore now, O LORD, please take my life from me, for **it is better for me to die than to live**." (verse 3)

God refuses (yet again) to kill Jonah, so Jonah finds a good vantage point where he can sulk, blast My Chemical Romance through his earbuds, and wait for God to change his mind and start with the Nineveh-destroying pyrotechnics already. It's hot sitting in the sun, so God throws him yet another bone:

Now **the LORD God appointed a plant and made it come up over Jonah**, that it might be a shade over his head, to save him from his discomfort. **So Jonah was exceedingly glad because of the plant**. (verse 6)

Shade and schadenfreude go pretty well together, but the Lord giveth and the Lord taketh away:

But when dawn came up the next day, God appointed **a worm that attacked the plant**, so that it withered. (verse 7)

Jonah's response, as with his response to everything, is to be a massive drama queen, railing at God for daring to kill the plant *just when he was getting used to being in the shade*. So God throws a bit more shade (get it? it's a pun) his way:

And the LORD said, "**You pity the plant, for which you did not labor**, nor did you make it grow, which came into being in a night and perished in a night. **And should not I pity Nineveh**, that great city, in which there are more than 120,000 persons who do not know their right hand from their left, **and also much cattle**?" (verses 10–11)

That's the very last line in the book of Jonah, and it might be the most anticlimactic line in all of the Bible: ". . . and also there were some cows!" Still, the point is clear: the cows in Nineveh didn't do anything wrong (aside from the whole methane thing), but they would have died along with everyone else had God nuked the place.[12] And—even more to the point—the presence of cattle suggests that Nineveh was a source of food to a lot of people. Sometimes it's hard to punish the guilty without punishing the innocent as well.

Spending a few minutes observing humanity in action, though, will confirm that very few of us like mercy unless we personally stand to benefit from it. Jonah was no exception—and the dude was a *prophet*.

I sure hope he was better at his side hustle.

"FLOATING AXE HEAD" IS THE NAME OF MY PROG ROCK BAND

In 2 Kings 6, Elisha and his apprentice prophetlings are building a big communal house for themselves on the banks of the Jordan River. (They've got some sort of

---

12. *Cow*lateral damage, am I right, folks? Am I right? I got a *moo*llion of them. Hey, where are you going?

Real Prophets of Jordan Shore thing going on.) It turns out at least one of them shouldn't quit his propheting gig to pursue a construction career:

> But as one was felling a log, **his axe head fell into the water**, and he cried out, "Alas, my master! **It was borrowed**." (verse 5)

Elisha says, "I'll get it!" but prophets of the Lord do *not* get their hands dirty:

> Then the man of God said, "Where did it fall?" When he showed him the place, he cut off a stick and threw it in there and **made the iron float**. And he said, "Take it up." So he reached out his hand and took it. (verses 6-7)

Daniel Reads Some Magic Graffiti

Like Jonah, the prophecy of Daniel is a *weird* book. It sprawls across multiple genres, two different languages, several narrators, and a few different canons. It's half Sunday school–ready narratives and half nightmarish prophecy; it switches between Hebrew and Aramaic almost at random; the stories are told by several different characters and veer from first to third person without warning; several of its anecdotes were too weird to even make it into Jewish or Protestant Bibles. So it's a bit of a hodgepodge. Daniel prophesies some, but he also survives some attempts on his life and solves a few mysteries around Babylon with his friends. (It's basically one talking dog short of being a Hanna-Barbera cartoon.) And, as you'll see, some of those mysteries are weirder than others.

Daniel 5 opens like this:

King Belshazzar made a great feast for a thousand of his lords and **drank wine in front of the thousand**. (verse 1)

Belshazzar is the king of Babylon, where Daniel and what's left of the once-great nation of Israel are in exile, and here he is *drinking wine in front of everyone.* (Leave it to royalty to imagine anyone would want to watch him get sloshed.) Mainly, though, the whole party is flagrantly sacrilegious, because

Then **they brought in the golden vessels that had been taken out of the temple**, the house of God in Jerusalem, and the king and his lords, his wives, and his concubines drank from them. They drank wine **and praised the gods of gold and silver, bronze, iron, wood, and stone**. (verses 3–4)

So what could have been a relatively wholesome alcohol-fueled orgy is turned into a profane mess when Belshazzar decides to put away Grandma's nice china and instead use the sacred goblets he stole from Israel's temple—all while *praising false gods.* This is *bad*, especially since we're in the Bible, where God makes a habit of getting involved in the affairs of mortals. And if you're waiting for a sign, things don't get much more ominous than this:

Immediately **the fingers of a human hand appeared and wrote on the plaster of the wall of the king's palace**, opposite the lampstand. And the king saw the hand as it wrote. (verse 5)

Belshazzar, like all of us, is terrified of PowerPoint presentations, so he turns into a cartoon:

Then the king's color changed, and his thoughts alarmed him; **his limbs gave way**, and **his knees knocked together**. (verse 6)

He has trouble reading the writing on the wall, though,[13] so he makes like a biblical king and calls in dozens of hack magicians, all of whom look at the thing and shrug. Fortunately, the queen knows a guy who's just *awesome* at solving spooky mysteries, and that guy just happens to be (surprise!) the guy whose name is the title of the book.

Belshazzar promises Daniel piles of wealth and power if he'll just read the words; Daniel says he's not interested in that stuff, but sure, he'll read it. Belshazzar says, "It's good news, right?" Daniel says, "Ha, nope":

"And this is the writing that was inscribed: **MENE, MENE, TEKEL, and PARSIN.** This is the interpretation of the matter: MENE, God has numbered the days of your kingdom and brought it to an end; TEKEL, you have been weighed in the balances and found wanting; PERES, your kingdom is divided and given to the Medes and Persians." (verses 25–28)

This all loses something in the translation, but **"Mene,"**

13. I, too, have trouble reading graffiti, because I am extremely white and, like, a thousand years old.

"Tekel," and "Parsin" are all money puns, suggesting that God knew the only way to get through to Belshazzar was by talking about wealth.[14] That would explain why he thought getting drunk out of the sacred vessels was such a good idea in the first place; it also explains why he straight-up ignores Daniel's refusal of wealth and power:

> Then Belshazzar gave the command, and **Daniel was clothed with purple, a chain of gold was put around his neck,** and a proclamation was made about him, that he should be the third ruler in the kingdom. (verse 29)

Daniel's newfound political power lasts about as long as you'd expect it to, given the prophecy he just made:

> That very night **Belshazzar the Chaldean king was killed.** And Darius the Mede received the kingdom, being about sixty-two years old. (verses 30–31)

GOOD THING THEY NOTICED BEFORE THEY SEALED UP THE TOMB

In the thirteenth chapter of 2 Kings, some guys are burying a dead man, and they figure, "Screw it, let's just get this job done and hit the links":

---

14. Donald C. Polaski, "Mene, Mene, Tekel, Parsin: Writing and Resistance in Daniel 5 and 6," *Journal of Biblical Literature* 123, no. 4 (2004): 649–69.

> And as a man was being buried, behold, a marauding band was seen and **the man was thrown into the grave of Elisha**, and as soon as the man touched the bones of Elisha, **he revived and stood on his feet**. (verse 21)

> So Elisha's body was so infused with God's spirit that it could restore corpses back to life. It would have been *really* cool if it could have restored *itself* back to life, but I guess it doesn't work that way.

Jesus vs. Haunted Pork

In the fourth chapter of Mark's gospel, Jesus and his disciples sail across the Sea of Galilee. It's an uneventful voyage, except for the part where a storm nearly kills them all, and Jesus tells the storm to cut it out, and it does, because he's Jesus. But as soon as they disembark, they come face-to-face with a prototypical horror movie trope:

> And when Jesus had stepped out of the boat, immediately there met him out of the tombs **a man with an unclean spirit**. (Mark 5:2)

He's not quite at the pea-soup-puking stage of things yet, but he *is* kind of a disaster:

> He **lived among the tombs**. And no one could bind him anymore, not even with a chain, for he had often been bound with

shackles and chains, but he wrenched the chains apart, and he broke the shackles in pieces. **No one had the strength to subdue him.** (verses 3–4)

As I'm sure you know, Jesus and demons don't get along super well, so he and this hot mess of a guy immediately start butting heads over whether human beings are appropriate playthings for supernatural entities:

And when he saw Jesus from afar, he ran and fell down before him. And crying out with a loud voice, he said, "**What have you to do with me, Jesus, Son of the Most High God?** I adjure you by God, do not torment me." **For he was saying to him, "Come out of the man, you unclean spirit!"** (verses 6–8)

My main takeaway here is that demons are incapable of taking hints, even when you're literally telling them exactly what you want ("**Come out of the man,**" etc.). In any case, if you've ever wondered where the horror movie cliché of asking demons their names comes from, wonder no more:

And Jesus asked him, "**What is your name?**" (verse 9a)

You can almost hear the gears turning in the demon's head as he admonishes himself, "Give him a *cool* name! Give him a *cool* name!"

He replied, "**My name is Legion**, for we are many." (verse 9b)

Nailed it.

Cool name or not, though, Legion is *super* not into giving this poor guy his body back, I assume because the big demon gala is coming up and he needs something trendy to wear to it—preferably made of flesh.[15] Hey, wait, what if there was a compromise that could make *everyone* happy?

> Now a great herd of pigs was feeding there on the hillside, and they begged him, saying, "**Send us to the pigs**; let us enter them." (verses 11–12)

"I would rather wear live pigs than go naked" sounds like the worst PETA campaign ever, but Jesus shrugs and says, "Fine, go in the pigs, I guess, you freaking weirdo," and what happens next is a graceful ballet of mass pig suicide:

> So he gave them permission. And **the unclean spirits came out and entered the pigs**; and the herd, numbering about two thousand, **rushed down the steep bank into the sea** and drowned in the sea. (verse 13)

This is great news, as long as you're not a fan of demons or pigs, or, more to the point, unless you were the owner of the pigs in question. Fortunately for Jesus, the swineherds get too freaked out to demand his insurance information:

> **The herdsmen fled** and told it in the city and in the country. (verse 14a)

The former demoniac, on the other hand, gets a happy ending:

---

15. Note my restraint in not making a Lady Gaga joke.

And they came to Jesus and saw **the demon-possessed man**, the one who had had the legion, sitting there, **clothed and in his right mind**, and they were afraid. (verse 15)

The locals are so overjoyed that—

They began to **beg Jesus to depart** from their region. (verse 17)

Just kidding. They can't deal with the whole thing, because exorcisms are freaky. Maybe that's part of why the ex-demoniac wants to get out of there:

As he was getting into the boat, the man who had been possessed with demons **begged him that he might be with him**. (verse 18)

He asks, essentially, for the standard "disciple" package, but Jesus is like, "Dude, don't try to make this something it isn't":

And he did not permit him but said to him, "**Go home to your friends** and tell them how much the Lord has done for you, and how he has had mercy on you." (verse 19)

. . . which, honestly, seems like all the work of being an apostle with none of the prestige. But at least he got some exorcise.

CHAPTER EIGHT

STRANGE FLESH

Incest and Outcest

In this chapter we're diving into the bottom of the cesspit, or the apotheosis of the cesspit, if you want to think of it that way. I dunno; you're the weirdo who's reading a chapter about incest in the Bible, so you tell me.

These stories mainly have to do with incest, but not quite all of them, which is why I had to make up a word for the subtitle. Nearly everything described here, it should be said, is condemned in Scripture, although not always in the same passages in which it's described, which has provided plenty of ammo to, presumably, the same people who think Stephen King is in favor of feeding children to cannibalistic clowns. Those who are genuinely disturbed that the Bible depicts this stuff can flip over to Leviticus for reassurance that God condemned all or most of it even then—though, fair warning, he probably condemned a lot of stuff you like as well. That's life—we can't *all* have our very specific preferences written into the Bible.

In any case, whether it approves of them or not, the Bible is riddled with incest and other depraved sex acts. They're particularly concentrated in Genesis, presumably because, at the beginning of time, it was hard to find a sex partner who *wasn't* a close relative. They're also scattered throughout the Bible, though, because, no matter how populous the world became, people's relatives continued to be unbelievably hot.

I've collected all but one of the Bible's worst (best?) sexy moments in this chapter for your reading pleasure. Some may accuse me of peddling puerile, pornographic smut, but you won't, because you know how the twenty-first century works: there's no market anymore for puerile, pornographic smut, because you can get that stuff for free, and in unlimited quantities, just by turning on your smartphone. No, this is a classy book, and you're a classy individual who reads classy books, because books are absolutely still relevant and vital in the age of the internet, and thank you for supporting hardworking authors and fine publishers.

Where was I, again? Oh yeah. Classy stuff. And incest.

Here we go!

Amnon and Tamar: Royal Families Have Basically Always Been Incestuous, but in This Story It's Bad

Remember a couple of chapters ago when I said that being named Tamar in the Bible is pretty much a guarantee that you're going to get raped? Here's some more proof.

In this story King David is getting old, and his various hormone-crazed sons and daughters are all doing the *Game of Thrones* thing, mainly with their crotches (not that there's another way to do it). He's got a son named Amnon and a daughter named (sigh) Tamar, and things between them are kind of like . . . this:

> Now Absalom, David's son, had **a beautiful sister, whose name was Tamar**. And after a time **Amnon, David's son, loved her**. (2 Samuel 13:1)

David, in case you forgot, is polygamous—the Bible mentions eight wives—so Tamar and Amnon are half siblings, not full siblings, which might make what's about to happen slightly less disgusting, depending, of course, on what you're disgusted by. Do keep your eye on that unpleasantly euphemistic word **"love,"** though—things get very un–Hallmark Channel, very fast.

The whole George Michael / Maeby scenario is starting to grate on Amnon:

> And Amnon was so tormented that **he made himself ill** because of his sister Tamar, for she was a virgin, and **it seemed impossible to Amnon to do anything to her**. (verse 2)

Which—wow, that's really the word choice we're going with here? **"It seemed impossible to Amnon to do anything to her"?** We've blown right past "Amnon didn't know how to talk to girls" to "He couldn't figure out how to slip her the D"? *Yeesh*.

Amnon thinks for a bit, scratches at his neckbeard, and decides to consult his cousin Jonadab, whose name sounds suspiciously like the alias of a Twitch streamer, and who knows all about the ladies, you see:

> Jonadab said to him, **"Lie down on your bed and pretend to be ill.** And when your father comes to see you, say to him,

'**Let my sister Tamar come and give me bread to eat**, and prepare the food in my sight, that I may see it and eat it from her hand.'" (verse 5)

It's the old pretend-to-be-sick-so-you-can-rape-your-sister strategy, which I believe is in the pickup artist handbook, right between peacocking and negging. Amnon pours some orange juice in the toilet, holds the thermometer up to a lightbulb, and yells, "Woman! Come make me a sammich!" (as one does). Tamar, doting sister that she is, dutifully hooks him up, and then:

But when she brought them near him to eat, he took hold of her and said to her, **"Come, lie with me, my sister."** (verse 11)

As we all know, the two steps to seducing a woman are to (1) act sick and pukey, and (2) actively remind her that you're blood relatives. For some reason, though, Tamar is not super enthusiastic about the proposed tryst:

She answered him, "No, my brother, do not violate me, for such a thing is not done in Israel; do not do this outrageous thing. As for me, where could I carry my shame? And as for you, you would be as one of the outrageous fools in Israel. Now therefore, **please speak to the king, for he will not withhold me from you.**" (verses 12–13)

You're in a *low* place when your go-to is "Please at least marry me before you incestuously rape me," but, well, the ancient world was not a great place to be a woman. Given what we know about Amnon—he can't talk to girls, he's obsessed with his sister, *she's responding to his proposition with a proposal*—you'd think this would be like winning the lottery for him. But of course you'd be wrong:

> But he would not listen to her, and being stronger than she, **he violated her and lay with her.** (verse 14)

And at this point, maybe the worst is over for Tamar, except of course Amnon decides to give her the I-just-raped-you-so-that-makes-you-a-slut treatment:

> **Then Amnon hated her with very great hatred**, so that the hatred with which he hated her was greater than the love with which he had loved her. And Amnon said to her, "Get up! Go!" (verse 15)

The denouement to this little escapade isn't pretty either. Maybe you remember the name Absalom from earlier in the pericope; he's Tamar's full brother, and it turns out he's *not* cool with her getting raped. He avenges her by murdering Amnon, which I'm honestly kind of fine with, since I was having trouble keeping the names "Absalom" and "Amnon" straight. This, in turn, leads to a big civil war where hundreds of people die, which is kind of the norm for a lot of ancient Israel's history but still isn't great.

ON STEPMOMS, ATTRACTIVE

In the fifth chapter of his first epistle to the Corinthians, St. Paul writes:

It is actually reported that there is sexual immorality among you, and of a kind that is not tolerated even among pagans, **for a man has his father's wife**. And you are arrogant! (verses 1–2a)

Evidently, some guy at the church in Corinth was walking in every Sunday morning, high-fiving the parishioners and shouting, "Dudes, I totally did it with my hot stepmom again!"

Greek playwright Aristophanes (who predates Paul's letters by a few centuries) supposedly coined the word *korinthiazomai*, which derives from the word "Corinth" and roughly translates as "to act like a man-slut."[1] He may have been onto something.

Swinging with Abram, Sarai, and Pharaoh

Hey, remember that guy who was sometimes named Abram and sometimes named Abraham? That guy that God promised to make into a great nation? That guy? Shortly after making that seminal (literally) vow, God asks him to pack up his things and move to the promised land. Like the nation of Israel after him, though, Abram has to make a quick pit stop in Egypt on the way there—easy enough, except as they cross into Egypt, he's like, "Whoops, I just remembered, my wife's hot":

1. Simon Hornblower, *The Greek World 479–323 B.C.* (Abingdon, United Kingdom: Routledge, 2011), 137.

When he was about to enter Egypt, he said to Sarai his wife, "I know that you are a woman beautiful in appearance, and when the Egyptians see you, they will say, 'This is his wife.' **Then they will kill me, but they will let you live.**" (Genesis 12:11–12)

"They will let you live" sounds pretty good, but **"they will kill me"** sounds less good, so Abram hatches a clever little scheme to avoid the whole "getting killed" thing:

"**Say you are my sister**, that it may go well with me because of you, and that my life may be spared for your sake." (verse 13)

Abram's expectations prove to be entirely accurate. Egypt was supposedly one of the cultural and scientific powerhouses of the ancient world, but the second the couple crosses its borders, "Wow, a hot girl!" becomes front-page news:

When Abram entered Egypt, the Egyptians saw that the woman was very beautiful. And when the princes of Pharaoh saw her, **they praised her to Pharaoh**. (verses 14–15a)

At the time, standard protocol for the "hot girl" scenario was apparently "Tell the king, immediately," and not something that would make sense, like "Get her phone number." Telling the king has the exact result you would expect:

And the woman was **taken into Pharaoh's house**. (verse 15b)

This was, presumably, just how things worked in the ancient world—if you're an eight or better, boom, you're in the king's harem. And if you have a husband, he's dead, because polygyny's cool, but polyandry? That's just *weird*.

While Sarai's off getting raped who-knows-how-many times, Abram's little white lie is working out pretty well for him:

> And **for her sake he dealt well with Abram**; and he had sheep, oxen, male donkeys, male servants, female servants, female donkeys, and camels. (verse 16)

Being his wife's pimp doesn't seem to bother Abram (could *you* turn down all that free livestock?), but God—party pooper that he is—is *not* cool with the situation:

> But the LORD afflicted Pharaoh and his house with **great plagues** because of Sarai, Abram's wife. (verse 17)

Unfortunately for Pharaoh, he's living in the Old Testament, and if there's one thing God enjoyed doing in the Old Testament, it was inflicting plagues on guys named "Pharaoh." Pharaoh is less than thrilled with Abram's deception:

> So Pharaoh called Abram and said, "What is this you have done to me? Why did you not tell me that she was your wife? Why did you say, 'She is my sister,' so that I took her for my wife? **Now then, here is your wife; take her, and go."** (verses 18–19)

So Sarai got raped, Pharaoh got plagued, but Abram made out pretty well—not only is he alive, but he's walking away with a bunch of free stuff. That might be why he fails to learn any sort of lesson from the experience and *pulls the exact same thing again*, eight chapters later (following his name change):

> **And Abraham said of Sarah his wife, "She is my sister."** And Abimelech king of Gerar sent and took Sarah. (Genesis 20:2)

This time around, he's passing through the Philistine town of Gerar, and he thinks, "Hmm, telling a king my wife is my sister worked out well last time; let's try it again!" Things go down about the same way the second time around: Sarah gets drafted into another harem; Abram gets free stuff. God, however, dispenses with the plagues and just cuts to the chase:

> But God **came to Abimelech in a dream by night** and said to him, "**Behold, you are a dead man** because of the woman whom you have taken, for she is a man's wife." (verse 3)

Abimelech, like Pharaoh before him, is not super thrilled about earning a spot on God's hit list, and tells Abraham as much. Abraham has this . . . jaw-dropping thing . . . to say in his own defense:

> "Besides, **she is indeed my sister, the daughter of my father though not the daughter of my mother**, and she became my wife." (verse 12)

Plot twist: turns out she *was* his sister! Abraham and Sarah were exactly as related as Amnon and Tamar, which . . . yay? I mean, I promised you incest in this chapter, so, there you go.

Oh, and then we get this insane bit of backstory:

"And when God caused me to wander from my father's house, I said to her, 'This is the kindness you must do me: **at every place to which we come, say of me, "He is my brother."**'" (verse 13)

So the "She's my sister!" thing wasn't a random improvisation; *it was Abraham's go-to move.* It's only recorded twice in Genesis,[2] but who knows how many times he pulled it—especially considering how well it worked out for him, *every single time*:

Then Abimelech **took sheep and oxen, and male servants and female servants, and gave them to Abraham**, and returned Sarah his wife to him. (verse 14)

So kids, I think the moral of the story here is "Pimp your wife out, under half-true pretenses, to as many despots as you can."

ON YOUR DAD'S POLITICAL AUTHORITY, FUN WAYS TO CHALLENGE

In 2 Samuel 16, when King David's son Absalom is intent on usurping his father's throne, he asks his friend Ahithophel how he can best establish his authority. Ahithophel gives him what *should* be the obvious answer: Have a lot of sex. Outside. With everyone watching.

Ahithophel said to Absalom, "**Go in to your father's concubines**, whom he has left to keep the house,

---

2. Unless you count when Abraham's son Isaac tries to pull the exact same stunt in chapter 26.

and all Israel will hear that you have made yourself a stench to your father, and the hands of all who are with you will be strengthened." So they **pitched a tent** for Absalom on the roof. And Absalom went in to his father's concubines in the sight of all Israel. (verses 21–22)

I'd absolutely take the time here to break down why this is such a powerful affront to David's authority, except I'm too busy giggling at the phrase **"pitched a tent."**

Jacob and Leah: Everyone Looks the Same in the Dark

The rape, deception, and incest doesn't stop with Abraham, though. If we flip forward nine chapters, we find the story of Abraham's grandson Jacob, who just really, really wanted to marry his cousin. And got what he wanted. Multiple times.

Jacob, for reasons that don't really come into this story, is on the run from his vengeful, murderous brother, and he does what any of us would do in that situation: crashes with his creepy uncle, Laban, and his hot female cousins. Actually, just *one* hot female cousin:

Now Laban had two daughters. The name of the older was Leah, and the name of the younger was Rachel. **Leah's eyes were weak**, but Rachel was beautiful in form and appearance. (Genesis 29:16–17)

It's not entirely clear what **"eyes were weak"** means, but commentators have suggested that it refers to ophthalmia, a condition that's not uncommon in dry, sandy regions like the Middle East,[3] and was apparently considered a *huge* defect in the ol' meat market back then.[4] The other possibility is that Leah was one of those "nerdy" girls from an '80s teen comedy, where you think she isn't hot until she finally takes off her Coke-bottle glasses and lets her hair down, and then, wait, *wow, she was hot the whole time.*

Either way, in an era when boning your cousin wasn't just a popular pastime but an inevitability, you can guess which cousin's pants Jacob has his eye on. When Laban asks him how he'd like to be compensated for all the freelance shepherd work he's doing for him, Jacob doesn't think twice:

> Jacob loved Rachel. And he said, **"I will serve you seven years for your younger daughter Rachel."** (verse 18)

Laban says "Cool cool cool, I see nothing creepy or dehumanizing about selling my daughter like a piece of meat," and Jacob dutifully puts in the seven years. When the time is up, though, Laban pulls the ol' switcheroo:

> So Laban gathered together all the people of the place and made a feast. But in the evening **he took his daughter Leah and brought her to Jacob**, and he went in to her. . . . **And in the morning, behold, it was Leah!** (verses 22–23, 25a)

---

3. Benjamin J. Gordon, MD, "Ophthamology in the Bible and the Talmud," *Archaeological Ophthamology* 9, no. 5 (1933): 751–88.

4. In fairness, eyes afflicted with ophthalmia *can* look pretty gross.

STRANGE FLESH

If you're wondering how *that* worked, presumably it was because brides were traditionally veiled in the ancient Near East,[5] and electric lights were (obviously) not a thing yet. Also, this being a wedding, it's safe to assume that everyone was pretty drunk, in addition to dizzy from dancing the Electric Slide very badly. Given all that, *every* wedding must have been a total crapshoot—you married your wife, took her to your pitch-dark tent, did the deed, and hoped no one was pulling a *Revenge of the Nerds* on you.

Jacob, understandably, confronts Laban about the whole business:

> And Jacob said to Laban, "What is this you have done to me? Did I not serve with you for Rachel? Why then have you deceived me?" Laban said, **"It is not so done in our country, to give the younger before the firstborn."** (verses 25b–26)

. . . which is a perfectly reasonable explanation, I *guess*, except it seems like Laban could have mentioned it *at literally any point in the last seven years.*

We might as well not mince words on this one: while it's hard to say exactly how "in" on the ruse Leah was, what she did technically amounted to rape, at least in the laws of a handful of modern countries. Jurisdictions including the United Kingdom,[6]

5. E.g., see Genesis 24:65, discussed in chapter 1, where Rebekah veils herself before meeting Isaac.
6. "Woman Who Posed as Man Jailed for Sex Assaults," BBC News, November 12, 2015, https://www.bbc.com/news/uk-england-34799692.

Israel,[7] and California[8] have all successfully prosecuted "rape by deception" cases, in which otherwise consensual sex occurred only because the victim was deceived about the perpetrator's identity. So Jacob just labored for seven years for the privilege of getting raped by his cousin, but then again, he *was* angling to purchase that other cousin like a side of beef, so my sympathy for him is a tad limited.

In any case, Laban is more than happy to make good on his original promise. Sort of:

> "Complete the week of this one, and we will give you the other also **in return for serving me another seven years.**" (verse 27)

It's sort of like how cable companies make you pay for Syfy, even though no one you've ever met or heard of actually watches Syfy. Jacob goes along with it, though, so I can only assume Rachel is *super* hot.

FUN WAYS TO CHALLENGE DAD'S AUTHORITY, PART 2

Genesis 35 contains the following aside:

> While Israel [Jacob] lived in that land, **Reuben went and lay with Bilhah his father's concubine**. And Israel heard of it. (verse 22a)

---

7. "Israel Jails Arab in 'Sex through Fraud' Case," Reuters, July 22, 2010, https://www.reuters.com/article/us-israel-sex-idUKTRE66L2PX20100722.

8. Lauren Blau, "Police Seek More Victims in 'Cure' Fraud: Man Charged with Getting Women to Have Sex as Treatment," *Los Angeles Times*, March 31, 1987, http://articles.latimes.com/1987-03-31/local/me-1458_1_orange-county-woman.

That's it. No context or anything, just, "Hey, bee tee dubs, Reuben did it with his dad's concubine." Fourteen chapters later, Israel (the guy formerly known as Jacob) disinherits him for doing it, but for the moment, the reader is mostly just left saying, "Uh . . . okay?"

As with Absalom earlier, this was primarily a means of asserting his authority over and above his father's—it was less about sex and more about power, as sex usually is. Still, Bilhah would have been about twice his age and the mother of two of his brothers, which is just . . . awkward. But you do you, Reuben. And by "you," I mean "your dad's concubine."

Lot, His Daughters, a Few Bottles of Wine, Date Rape, Etc.

You remember Lot, right? He was Abraham's nephew, and he lived in Sodom—y'know, the place God destroyed for being into weird sex and/or failing to show hospitality? I touched on this in chapter 3, but in case you forgot, some angels came to warn Lot of the impending destruction, his neighbors tried to gang-rape said angels, and he tried to convince them to gang-rape his daughters instead (like you do). Anyway, the good ("good") news is that his daughters end up getting revenge. Of a sort. I guess.

To pick up where we left off, Lot and fam manage to just barely escape Sodom without getting destroyed. They're warned to (literally) run for the hills without looking back, but Lot's wife *does* look back and as a result becomes a "pillar of salt." That might seem like a weirdly specific thing to get turned into, but it turns out vaguely humanoid salt formations are actually fairly common in the area surrounding the Dead Sea, where Sodom was supposedly located. Most of these formations are also ten feet tall, which makes it unlikely they were actually formed from human women, but who knows?[9]

Anyway, the upshot is that Lot and his daughters end up bachin' it in a cave:

> Now Lot went up out of Zoar and lived in the hills with his two daughters, for he was afraid to live in Zoar. **So he lived in a cave with his two daughters.** (Genesis 19:30)

I guess this makes them literal cavemen, especially given how close we are to the beginning of time here, but it turns out it's not all laugh tracks and Fruity Pebbles, especially not once his daughters' biological clocks start ticking:

> And the firstborn said to the younger, "Our father is old, and there is not a man on earth to come in to us after the manner of all the earth. Come, let us make our father drink wine, and **we will lie with him**, that we may preserve offspring from our father." (verses 31–32)

So they're conspiring to date-rape their own dad, which I guess is arguably less horrific than his earlier attempt to get them gang-raped, but not by a whole lot. Some commentators have suggested the daughters are under the impression that the whole world—not only Sodom and Gomorrah—has been destroyed,

---

9. Frederick G. Clapp, "Geology and Bitumens of the Dead Sea Area, Palestine and Transjordan," *AAPG Bulletin* 20, no. 7 (1936): 881–909.

and they're the literal last people on earth,[10] which would make this plan a *bit* more understandable. Meanwhile, the ancient rabbinic text Genesis Rabbah argues that the daughters knew (*somehow*) that they were the ancestors of the coming Messiah, and that raping their own father seemed like the best way to ensure that *that* whole thing happened.[11] Which, sure, why not.

In any case, they play a few rounds of wine pong, get Dad good and sloshed, and boink his brains out:

> So they **made their father drink wine** that night. And **the firstborn went in and lay with her father**. He did not know when she lay down or when she arose. (verse 33)

Lot is apparently only good for one roll in the hay before he passes out, so the second daughter has to repeat the process the following night. Both daughters manage to conceive sons, and then we find out this whole narrative was just an elaborate "your momma" joke:

> The firstborn bore a son and called his name Moab. **He is the father of the Moabites** to this day. The younger also bore a son and called his name Ben-ammi. **He is the father of the Ammonites** to this day. (verses 37–38a)

Those two nations that spend a large chunk of the Old Testament warring against Israel? Turns out they're the result of *inbreeding!* Ha, take *that*, Moabites and Ammonites!

---

10. Johanna Stiebert, *First-Degree Incest in the Hebrew Bible: Sex in the Family* (New York: Bloomsbury, 2016), 158.

11. Genesis Rabbah, 58:1.

That's . . . that's it. That's the whole joke.

So, if you thought the pettiness of Middle Eastern politics was a new thing—nah, that stuff literally goes back to prehistory. But I'm sure whatever peace accord they're working on right now will smooth things over once and for all.

THE PART ABOUT SHEEP SEX YOU'VE ALL BEEN WAITING FOR

I know what you're thinking: "The Bible seems like a cool book, but can it teach me how to control ovine reproduction like some sort of dark, all-powerful sheep god?" Well, I got you, fam.

In Genesis 30, after Jacob works fourteen years to "earn" Laban's two daughters—i.e., Jacob's cousins, i.e., Jacob's wives—Jacob agrees to stay on as a herdsman for Laban in exchange for "every speckled and spotted sheep and every black lamb, and the spotted and speckled among the goats." Laban tries to cheat him by pre-removing most of the stock he describes, but Jacob gets the last laugh in the end, by *magically controlling sheep sex:*

> Then Jacob took fresh sticks of poplar and almond and plane trees, and peeled white streaks in them, exposing the white of the sticks. He **set the sticks that he had peeled in front of the flocks in the troughs**, that is, the watering places, where the flocks came to drink. And

since they bred when they came to drink, the flocks bred in front of the sticks **and so the flocks brought forth striped, speckled, and spotted**. (Genesis 30:37–39)

This move was almost definitely motivated by an ancient superstition, not some sort of profound knowledge of sheep reproduction, and even most of the rabbinic tradition agrees that Jacob prospered due to a miracle of God and not tainted sheep water. On the other hand, at least one commentator has suggested that recent advances in epigenetics imply that Jacob was legitimately onto something here.[12] So who knows.

The Nephilim: There's Really No Good Place for This So I'm Going to Stick It Here[13]

I mentioned this briefly in chapter 2, but I might as well say it again: Noah's Flood was *far* weirder than you learned in Sunday school. It ends, as we saw, with possible father-rape, and it starts with . . . angel-on-human sex.

(Maybe.)

In the lead-up to the Flood, the author tries to explain God's motivation for destroying the earth, and he starts with . . . this:

When man began to multiply on the face of the land and

---

12. Joshua Backon, "Jacob and the Spotted Sheep: The Role of Prenatal Nutrition on Epigenetics of Fur Color," *Jewish Bible Quarterly* 36, no. 4 (2008): 263–65.
13. Heh.

daughters were born to them, **the sons of God** saw that the daughters of man were attractive. And they **took as their wives** any they chose. (Genesis 6:1–2)

People have been arguing over the exact meaning of these two verses pretty much since the moment they were written. There are two main schools of thought: either (1) this is a passage about righteous people intermarrying with wicked people (i.e., the boring interpretation), or (2) this is a passage about *fallen angels raping human women* (i.e., the *awesome* interpretation). As I've always been firmly on the side of awesomeness, you can probably guess which interpretation I prefer. It's not for nothing, either—the idea that **"sons of God"** means "angels" appears to be borne out in the context, since this intermarrying results in *babies who are superheroes*:

The **Nephilim** were on the earth in those days, and also afterward, when the sons of God came in to the daughters of man and they bore children to them. These were **the mighty men who were of old**, the men of renown. (verse 4)

"Nephilim" is a word with a fairly obscure origin; some scholars suggest it comes from the Hebrew word *naphal*, the verb for "to fall" (as in "fallen angel"), while others argue it comes from an Aramaic word for "giant."[14] So the only possible interpretation here is that *angels raped human women and had babies who were superhero giants.*

---

14. Kevin P. Sullivan, *Wrestling with Angels: A Study of the Relationship between Angels and Humans in Ancient Jewish Literature and the New Testament* (Leiden, Netherlands: Brill, 2004), 198.

The Bible is *awesome*.

Admittedly, there are plenty of people who disagree with the fun interpretation of this passage. Modern Orthodox Judaism rejects it,[15] and even Christian heavy hitters like St. Augustine[16] and John Calvin[17] insisted that "sons of God" refers only to God-fearing human beings. If they were right, though, this would be news to at least one of the authors of the New Testament—namely Jude, who was likely Jesus' biological half brother,[18] and who wrote in his epistle:

> And the **angels which kept not their first estate, but left their own habitation**, he hath reserved in everlasting chains under darkness unto the judgment of the great day. Even as Sodom and Gomorrha, and the cities about them in like manner, giving themselves over to fornication, and **going after strange flesh**, are set forth for an example, suffering the vengeance of eternal fire. (Jude vv. 6–7 KJV)

It's hard to say for certain that Jude is referring to Genesis 6 here, but he seems to take it for granted that angels (1) left heaven, and (2) went after **"strange flesh."** You have to go pretty far out of your way to avoid the "angels did it with human women" interpretation.

Extracanonical books get even clearer about this sort of thing. The Book of Enoch (attributed to the man who is said to have

---

15. Medieval Rabbi Rashi, for instance, strongly preferred the translation "sons of the nobles" to the more literal "sons of God."

16. Augustine, *City of God*, 22.

17. John Calvin, *Commentaries on the First Book of Moses Called Genesis*, 6:1.

18. David A. deSilva, *The Jewish Teachers of Jesus, James, and Jude: What Earliest Christianity Learned from the Apocrypha and Pseudepigrapha* (Oxford: Oxford University Press, 2012), 45.

"walked with God, and [then] he was not, for God took him," in Genesis 5:24) describes the strange case of the Nephilim as follows:

> And it came to pass when the children of men had multiplied that in those days were born unto them beautiful and comely daughters. And **the angels, the children of the heaven, saw and lusted after them**, and said to one another: "Come, let us choose us wives from among the children of men and beget us children." And Semjâzâ, who was their leader, said unto them: "I fear ye will not indeed agree to do this deed, and I alone shall have to pay the penalty of a great sin." And they all answered him and said: "**Let us all swear an oath,** and all bind ourselves by mutual imprecations not to abandon this plan but to do this thing." (1 Enoch 6:1–4)

So, according to Enoch, not only did angels leave heaven to chase after human tail, they pulled an *American Pie* and swore a sacred oath to *all* do it, possibly by prom night. It's hard to argue with that (especially given the potential for endless direct-to-DVD sequels). It's also worth noting that the Book of Enoch, while excluded from Scripture by Catholic, Protestant, and Eastern Orthodox Christians, *is* considered canonical by the Ethiopian Orthodox Tewahedo Church, and I don't want to argue too much with those guys, since they (probably) have the ark of the covenant,[19] and I'm *super* not a fan of getting hemorrhoids and/or my face melted off.

---

19. Graham Hancock, *Sign and the Seal: The Quest for the Lost Ark of the Covenant* (New York: Simon and Schuster, 1993), 15.

CONCLUSION

Probably the Most Depraved
Passage in All of the Bible

You've made it.

You've arrived at the most violent, depraved story in the Bible, one so *Game of Thrones*-y that I thought it deserved its own chapter. Why are you even reading this, you sicko? Stay away from my kids.

We've talked about the book of Judges several times already—it's the one with Samson, Jephthah, Ehud, Jael, and Deborah—and much of it belongs in a book like this, since it's filled with weird, twisted stuff. What I haven't mentioned explicitly is that Judges presents itself, fundamentally, as an argument for the necessity of a united Israelite monarchy. There's a refrain to it that shows up a few times in the later chapters, and it goes like this:

> In those days there was no king in Israel. **Everyone did what was right in his own eyes.** (Judges 17:6)

And just in case that sounds like some sort of libertarian paradise, the author concludes the book with several chapters on what Israel was like when everyone got to make up his or her own moral code, and it ain't pretty. Probably the worst of these chapters opens like this:

> In those days, **when there was no king in Israel**, a certain
> Levite was sojourning in the remote parts of the hill country of
> Ephraim, who **took to himself a concubine** from Bethlehem
> in Judah. (19:1)

If you're unfamiliar with what a **concubine** is, the short answer is that it's the ancient equivalent of a live-in girlfriend—sort of a "we don't need a marriage license to be committed" kind of thing. (This was often because the woman came from a lower social class than the man, making marriage impossible under the norms of the time.)[1] It ain't all sunshine in Cohabitation Land, though:

> But she became angry with him, **went back to her father's house**
> in Bethlehem, and stayed there four months. (verse 2 GNT)

And if you're thinking, "This guy sounds like kind of human garbage," congrats on picking up on the subtext. Anyway, he goes to get her back, only to find out that her father likes him a whole lot more than she does:

> And when the girl's father saw him, he came with joy to meet
> him. And **his father-in-law, the girl's father, made him stay**,

---

1. Louis M. Epstein, "The Institution of Concubinage Among the Jews," *Proceedings of the American Academy for Jewish Research* 6 (1934–35): 153–88.

and he remained with him three days. So they ate and drank and spent the night there. (verses 3b–4)

This . . . goes on for longer than you might expect:

And on the fourth day they arose early in the morning, and he prepared to go, but the girl's father said to his son-in-law, **"Strengthen your heart with a morsel of bread, and after that you may go."** (verse 5)

And it just keeps going:

So the two of them sat and ate and drank together. And the girl's father said to the man, "Be pleased to spend the night, and let your heart be merry." **And when the man rose up to go, his father-in-law pressed him, till he spent the night there again.** (verses 6–7)

Are you skimming yet?

And on the fifth day he arose early in the morning to depart. And the girl's father said, "Strengthen your heart and wait until the day declines." So they ate, both of them. And when the man and his concubine and his servant rose up to depart, his father-in-law, the girl's father, said to him, "Behold, now the day has waned toward evening. Please, spend the night. Behold, the day draws to its close. **Lodge here and let your heart be merry, and tomorrow you shall arise early in the morning for your journey, and go home."** (verses 8–9)

All of this is essentially irrelevant to the story, by the way. It's just sort of *there*, possibly as an extended gag about how in-laws are the worst.[2] Eventually, though, the Levite and his concubine manage to escape the sucking vortex of his father-in-law's hospitality:

> But the man would not spend the night. **He rose up and departed** and arrived opposite Jebus (that is, Jerusalem). (verse 10a)

Because of the late start, they have to stay overnight in Gibeah, where they have the exact opposite problem they had at her father's house:

> And he went in and **sat down in the open square of the city**, for **no one took them into his house to spend the night**. (verse 15b)

That part will be familiar to anyone who remembers the story of the angels in Sodom from chapter 3. Remember Sodom? That place that got destroyed for being inhospitable? The parallels won't end here either.

Things start to look up, for a moment, when a lone stranger takes them into his home:

> And behold, an old man was coming from his work in the field at evening. . . . And the old man said, **"Peace be to you; I will care for all your wants. Only, do not spend the night in the square."** (verses 16a, 20)

---

2. Am I right, folks? Am I right? [*bowtie spins, boutonniere squirts seltzer*]

But guess what's next. Just guess! That's right, it's this damned[3] thing again:

> As they were making their hearts merry, behold, the men of the city, worthless fellows, **surrounded the house, beating on the door**. And they said to the old man, the master of the house, "Bring out the man who came into your house, **that we may know him**." (verse 22)

There's that old-timey expression **"know him"** again, which you'll recall is a charmingly awkward euphemism for sex—or, in this case, rape, since the Levite is less than enthusiastic about the proposed encounter. Again, this is exactly what we saw in Genesis, but the old man apparently never read Genesis—or, if he did, he learned the *exact wrong thing* from it:

> And the man, the master of the house, went out to them and said to them, "No, my brothers, do not act so wickedly; since this man has come into my house, do not do this vile thing. **Behold, here are my virgin daughter and his concubine.** Let me bring them out now. **Violate them and do with them what seems good to you**, but against this man do not do this outrageous thing." (verses 23–24)

Yep, it's the same old "don't rape my guest, rape some women instead." But while Lot's attempt to pimp out his daughters in Genesis was thwarted by the angels, there's a disappointing lack

---

3. If you're offended by this, please know that I'm using the word "damned" quite literally here—that is, this sort of thing is condemned by God. Also know that my first draft used an f-word. Which I also meant literally.

of angels here, and so the men in the room actually manage to go through with the plan. Well, halfway, anyway:

> But the men would not listen to him. **So the man seized his concubine and made her go out to them.** (verse 25a)

Quick reminder that this guy just spent a week getting his girlfriend back, and now he's throwing her out the door like a T-bone to some rabid dogs. Things go about as well for her as you might expect:

> And they knew her and abused her all night until the morning. And **as the dawn began to break, they let her go.** (verse 25b)

(Which was thoughtful of them.)

The Levite, meanwhile, gets a good night's sleep, enjoys his complimentary continental breakfast, then steps out to grab the paper and maybe also check on his raped-and-beaten girlfriend:

> And her master rose up in the morning, and when he opened the doors of the house and went out to go on his way, **behold, there was his concubine lying at the door of the house, with her hands on the threshold**. He said to her, "Get up, let us be going." **But there was no answer.** (verses 27–28a)

Rude.

Certain commentators have read a great deal into the choice of words here. The author doesn't even address the question of whether she's alive;[4] all he tells us is that she says nothing. Actually, she doesn't speak once in the entire passage, and this appears to be a stylistic choice as well, since she's not afforded a voice in the culture either.[5] Even on her best days, she's been treated like a piece of meat, and that's about to get a lot more literal. Also a lot more slasher-movie-y.

> Then he put her on the donkey, and the man rose up and went away to his home. And when he entered his house, **he took a knife, and taking hold of his concubine he divided her, limb by limb, into twelve pieces**, and sent her throughout all the territory of Israel. (verses 28b–29)

Once again, there's no mention here of her dying—or even of her boyfriend bothering to take a pulse before he starts butchering her. It's likely, of course, that she died the night before, or on the ride home—and, I mean, she's definitely dead *now*—but again, the emphasis seems to be on how little concern anyone has for her as a human being. In any case, FedExing her to Israel's twelve tribes seems to elicit the reaction he was looking for:

> And all who saw it said, "**Such a thing has never happened** or been seen from the day that the people of Israel came up out of the land of Egypt until this day." (verse 30a)

---

4. The Greek Septuagint inserts "for she was dead" right after "there was no answer" in verse 28, but it's not present in the original Hebrew.
5. Madipoane J. Masenya, "Without a Voice, with a Violated Body: Re-reading Judges 19 to Challenge Gender Violence in Sacred Texts," *Missionalia: Southern African Journal of Missiology* 40, no. 3 (2012): 205–16.

. . . which, I mean, one would *hope*.

This is one of those moments where I wish I could read a character's mind. "How can I alert Israel to the roving bands of gang rapists? I know, I'll send them part of my dismembered girlfriend!" I mean, presumably, he includes a note or something, but it seems like the note could have done the job on its own. Am I the crazy one here?

Still, the plan works, and by "works" I mean it causes a civil war to break out, followed by another round of mass rape, because, sure, that's exactly how I'd recommend solving the problem. Then the whole thing concludes with this familiar refrain:

> In those days there was no king in Israel. **Everyone did what was right in his own eyes.** (21:25)

So . . . yay?

/ / /

Recently, as my father did with me years ago, I've been reading the Bible with my six-year-old daughter. Like me, she's drawn to its strangest stories (her favorites so far are Elisha's murder-bears and Nebuchadnezzar's adventures eating grass); at the end of each one, she'll laugh, shake her head, say, "That's weird," and ask for more. Eventually, if I continue to oblige, we'll come around to stories like this one.

I'm not sure what I'll tell her when we do.

I've been pretty deliberate with the structure of this book, working my way up from fairly innocuous stuff like poop jokes to this story of rape, murder, and dismemberment here at the end. If there *is* a point to it all, it's this: The Bible contains many, many things that little old ladies will tell you are *inappropriate for children*, and that's because the Bible, fundamentally, isn't *for* children. The Bible, talking donkeys and all, was written for real people, in the real world, dealing with real evil. The Bible talks about butts because God cares about butts; it talks about sin, because . . . God cares about sin.

"Sin," of course, is a word that's been so overused that it's hard to quite understand what it is at its worst—which, I suppose, is why we need stories like the one about the Levite's concubine. Sin isn't just saying naughty words or looking at dirty pictures; it's a sickness that infects us all and allows things like rape and murder to occur. It's the strong exploiting the weak, and it both threatens and calls out to each of us.

Maybe that's kind of a heavy way to end the book, but evil is inescapably *real*, and for the writer—whether we're talking about the writers of Scripture or . . . *me*—the only real question is what to *do* with evil's reality. Do we laugh about it, or mourn it? Rage against it, or deny it? Just stare at it stoically? *Celebrate it?*

You all know which way *I* chose to take things, but ultimately, the preference on this seems to be a generational thing. In my lifetime I've seen the early pearl-clutching over the mild anarchy of *The Simpsons*, which eventually gave way to the cheerful nihilism of *South Park*, which arguably led directly to 4chan's habit of giggling at Nazis and pedophilia. You can, in turn, draw a straight line from the latter to the current rise of white nationalism, which seems to have effectively reminded everyone that "LOL, nothing matters!" seems like a hilarious aesthetic until it escapes out into the real world.

I found it difficult, as I was putting this book together, to keep the current trend toward aesthetic backpedaling—from "Haha, offensive stuff is hilarious!" to "Oops, we just remembered *why* that stuff was offensive"—out of my head. I am a famously chill dude, but there will always be the knowledge in the back of my mind that my daughters, as daughters, are statistically more likely than average to end up raped and dismembered somewhere. When I told my six-year-old that no one should touch her body without her permission, she smiled wide and announced, *"Everyone* has permission to touch my body!" I can teach her the Bible, and I can teach her the idea of consent, but I can't teach her things that come only from experience—like how much pain sin can cause.

Ultimately, no matter how libertine or prudish people become, evil has a habit of continuing to exist, and no system of philosophy or theology seems able to give a universally satisfying answer *why*. The so-called problem of evil—"How can an all-powerful, all-knowing, just God allow evil to exist?"— remains just as unanswered today as when Epicurus first posed it in 300 BC.[6] There *are* a few tentative answers in the Bible, if you look for them: maybe evil is rebellion against God (see Genesis 3); maybe evil is just one tool God uses to create ultimate good (see Genesis 50); maybe punishing evil is how God chooses to make his goodness known (see Romans 9). The Bible as a whole never really gives a simple, definitive answer to the question, though, other than to say that, when we suffer, God suffers with us (2 Corinthians 1:5)—and that slowly, somehow, all of the suffering is being undone.

---

6. John Hospers, *An Introduction to Philosophical Analysis* (Abingdon-on-Thames: Routledge, 1990), 310.

Early in the prophecy of Isaiah—amid a litany of oracles foretelling the military destruction of Jerusalem—the prophet writes this:

> He shall judge between the nations,
>> and shall decide disputes for many peoples;
> and **they shall beat their swords into plowshares**,
>> and their spears into pruning hooks;
> nation shall not lift up sword against nation,
>> **neither shall they learn war anymore**. (Isaiah 2:4)

I know what you're about to say: "I could think of something *a million times more awesome* to turn swords into than a stupid plow, like maybe a throne that doubles as a coatrack"—and (1) sure, I can see where you're coming from, (2) you own way too many swords, and (3) please at least *try* to appreciate the symbolism here, you uncultured swine. A sword—an instrument of death—is being turned into a tool for the cultivation of food—an instrument of life. Death itself will be turned into life. The evil will be reversed.

Even the Levite's concubine—raped, murdered, carved up like a side of beef—will one day be put back together. Not *sewn* together like a Frankenstein monster, but *restored*—healed, made alive, and given justice for the wrongs done to her.

We'll finally learn her name. We'll finally hear her speak.

Kings will fall on their knees to listen.

ACKNOWLEDGMENTS

The book you hold in your hands, like all books, is the work of far more people than just the guy who got his name on the cover. (To be clear, though, I'm not sharing the cover. It's comfy there.) This particular book has taken a long and tortuous route from conception to publication, which I will now relate to anyone who is interested in reading even more words that I wrote.

In the first place, at the risk of sounding like a Grammy winner (the lowest of all life-forms), I should probably thank God. In the summer of 2013, when I had decided to Get Serious About Writing, I was working on some pitches for Cracked.com. (Mind you, this was back when *Cracked* was actually worth reading—before they were bought out by a conglomerate who fired their editorial staff and transformed them into a clickbait factory.) *Cracked*, at the time, specialized in articles with titles like "6 _____ You Won't Believe Are _____," or "5 _____That Are Secretly _____." The articles they published, over-the-top titles aside, were of extremely high quality—top-notch writing, laugh-out-loud funny, deeply informative, meticulously sourced. I couldn't wait to write one, but I found that ideas were few and far between.

Since the pieces were united in theme, not content per se, they weren't the sort of thing you could build with mere research; you kind of just had to find factoids bouncing around inside your own head that you could link together with a common thread. It wasn't super easy.

Fortunately, the best ideas tend to pop into my head randomly while I'm waiting in line to kneel at the ol' Communion rail. You can impart spiritual significance to that if you want, or you could brush it aside as a mix of having my head in a contemplative space and walking around a bit. What I know for sure is that standing in line for the Eucharist every week that summer left me with a handful of pretty good ideas for *Cracked* articles, one of which eventually became "6 Filthy Jokes You Won't Believe Are from the Bible." (You can still find it at Cracked.com, if you're interested.)

When I first pitched the article, *Cracked*'s editors, among them Dan O'Brien and Kristi Harrison, were merciless. There were many, many rounds of repitching and revising, but for whatever reason, I stuck with it, and ultimately what emerged from the proverbial kiln was a piece I thought we could all be proud of. What I wasn't prepared for was how the piece was going to blow up. Among other things, I was seeing my name in Australian newspapers the next day, which was a little wild. The article still ranks as the most successful thing I've ever written, which isn't surprising considering my main other thing is literary horror novels about mopey English majors, but still.

It was, however, Holly Schmidt of book packager Hollan Publishing who first convinced me that the article had the potential to be expanded into a book. My time with Holly as my agent/ producer/editor/etc. didn't work out in the end (mainly because I was an absolute noob to the publishing industry and had no clue what I was doing), but her tutelage helped me outline and sharpen the idea for the book into something quasi-sensical. Meanwhile, the existence of my halfway-book-deal helped land me a steady gig at Christ and Pop Culture, a crucible that gave me both space to hone my style as a humorist and invaluable exposure to people who were on the same wavelength as me.

After my contract with Hollan expired, I assumed the project was dead in the water and I was doomed forever to publish indulgent psychological thrillers that would win awards but sell zero copies, until I was contacted out of nowhere by Todd Hains of Lexham Press. Under the guidance of Todd and his coworker Elliot Ritzema, *Murder-Bears* began to take shape. It was Todd and Elliot who convinced me I could be funny while still being vulnerable and credible, and the book would absolutely not exist without them. In the end, the project was killed once again by one of Lexham's execs, but I remain eternally grateful to Todd and Elliot, who fought in vain to save it.

After the second deal on the book had fallen through, I was left alone, holding on to a completed manuscript that seemingly nobody wanted, but one soul rescued me from the Slough of Despond: author K. B. Hoyle, who is a dear friend and one of my all-time favorite people, and to whom I owe (rough estimate) about 79.453 percent of my writing success. Had she not given me the kick in the butt I needed to get off the couch and start pitching the book again (which I actually did mainly on Twitter, so I guess I didn't need to get off the couch after all, which I'm pretty annoyed to realize just now), it would probably still be sitting in a folder in my computer, collecting dust, or corruptions, or whatever digital files collect. But yeah, K. B.'s cool. You should buy all of her books.

Of course, all of K. B.'s encouragement and all of my relentless, extremely eloquent tweeting would have meant nothing had Beth Adams of HarperCollins Christian Publishing not noticed me among the tweeting masses, fallen in love with my manuscript, and become a tireless advocate for it. Thanks to Beth, what could have been another failed project for the ol' dustbin has become my "Big Five" debut, which I admit I am at least a little thrilled about. I have endless gratitude toward Beth, both for believing in my book and for defending it fearlessly against the pearl-clutchers-that-be. Many thanks also to Meaghan Porter and Kevin Harvey, who copyedited the manuscript and reminded me that the made-up contraction "y'know" is, y'know, only funny so many times.

Having told that whole story, I should probably also thank everyone who taught me the Bible, thus making this book possible: My parents; my teachers at Lincoln, Nebraska's own Trinity Lutheran Elementary School; my pastors and Sunday school teachers at Lincoln's Faith Orthodox Presbyterian Church; Bart Moseman; Mike Hsu; Bryan Dahlberg; Deborah Warner; Chris Tiews; Chris Hall; Ryan Cortright; Phil Moldenhauer; and many others. Thank you all for showing me that the Bible was also for the troublemakers in the back row like me. Further, thanks to all my friends and colleagues who reviewed the manuscript and told me ~~how mind-blowingly awesome it was~~ how it could be improved: Laura Lundgren, Michelle Gourley, Wesley Walker, Amanda Scoggins, Scott Garbacz, Andrea Humphries, Richard Clark, Olivia Ard, Josh Lewis, Emily Dixon, Daniel Jones, and anyone else I'm forgetting.

Finally, all the thanks in the world must go to my wife, Julia, who I don't think really understands *why* I need to do the things

I do, but at least understands *that* I need to do them and works tirelessly to provide me the space and time to write. Thanks also to my young daughter, Lucy, who I hope isn't mad at me when she finds out I mentioned her in this book, and also my even younger daughter, Zoe, who I hope isn't mad at me when she finds out I *didn't* mention her in this book. Except I just mentioned her, so maybe we're good? I have no idea.

There are, of course, countless others whom I could thank, but I want this section to be at least somewhat shorter than the book itself, so I'll cut it off here. This is the end of the words, and the world is a beautiful place full of mystery and magic (and murder-bears and moonshine and mayhem), so why don't you put down the book, go outside, and discover something awesome?

Tell me what you find. We'll compare notes.

ABOUT THE AUTHOR

Luke T. Harrington is the only boy who could ever reach you. He's the son of a preacher man. He's also a humorist, podcaster, and award-winning novelist. His debut novel, *Ophelia, Alive*, won a 2016 IPPY, and his work has appeared in publications including *Cracked*, *BuzzFeed*, and *Christianity Today*. Other projects include *Project CoNarrative*, a collaborative multimedia experiment with bestselling author K. B. Hoyle, and *Changed My Mind with Luke T. Harrington*, his podcast where he interviews people who have changed their minds about big, important things. He lives in Wisconsin with his wife and two daughters.